truth on fire

truth on fire

the message of galatians

13370

clark h. pinnock

baker book house
grand rapids, michigan

Copyright © 1972 by
Baker Book House Company

ISBN: 0-8010-6927-0
Library of Congress Catalog Card Number: 72-85672

Printed in the United States of America

preface

Paul's Epistle to the Galatians is spiritual dynamite. Its message has ignited theological revolutions and reformations. Martin Luther called the letter his own epistle "to whom I have plighted my troth." For he found in it the theological principles which were to transform his life and ground his mighty faith. During his reforming ministry, he undertook series of lectures on the epistle, the text of which has had a deep effect on an unnumbered host of believers ever since.

Luther treasured Galatians highly because it gets right to the heart of what the Christian faith is all about. It sets forth salvation by the free grace of God without human works. It draws our attention to the complete sufficiency of Jesus Christ and the adequacy of simple faith as an acceptable and proper response to the gospel. The question it answers is a perennial one: Are we saved by believing or achieving? Do we rest on human accomplishments or on the finished work of Christ on the cross for salvation? This is a question Paul, Luther, and all of us must face. There are, in the last analysis, only two religions. One calls on men to impress God with their own deeds, and one demands that they renounce all such pretensions and cast themselves on God's unmerited favor in Christ. Even God's people are in constant danger of forgetting the beautiful simplicity of this alternative. Galatians was written to remind us of it.

What purpose lay behind Paul's writing of this epistle? Primarily he was concerned that the Galatian believers not lose their grip on the true gospel and forsake it (1:6; 5:2). False teachers were operating among the congregations, unsettling them and subverting gospel truth (1:7; 5:10). The situation urgently called for a vigorous defense of the gospel.

The material in Galatians divides roughly into three blocks. Two chapters each are devoted to three subjects: *truth, salvation, holiness.* The truth question is handled in the first two chapters. The presence of these false teachers put the Galatians in a state of confusion. They faced a dilemma so familiar to us in our day of religious pluralism. Here you had two sets of teachers, Paul and the Judaizers, each claiming divine authority, yet contradicting each other. Whom were the Galatians to believe? It was the question of authority in religion. Where does it lie? Who or what has the right to command our obedience? To whom has God delegated His authority? Paul answered the question for the Galatians by asserting his authority as an apostle of Jesus Christ (1:1, 11-12, 15-16). In order to prove that his authority derived from the risen Lord and not from any human source, even the Jerusalem church, Paul develops an argument from history. The facts themselves show that Paul is a special emissary of Jesus Christ, and therefore one to whom the Galatians ought to pay heed.

With the deep ferment in contemporary theology and the rise of many religious cults, the question of authority is a most critical one for us today. People are bombarded with a bewildering number of contradictory opinions and speculations, each claiming some prominent individual in support of it and advancing reasons to defend it. Paul's answer can help us today. The church of God is built on the foundation of the apostles and prophets (Eph. 2:20). It is an *apostolic* church. It bases its teachings, not on human ideas and traditions, but on the teachings of its Lord's apostles. The apostles as the messengers, witnesses, and authorized representatives of the crucified and risen Lord are first in the church (I Cor. 12:28; Eph. 4:11). The apostles are the irreplaceable foundation stones of the church, the cornerstone and keystone of which is Christ Himself.

Many readers of Galatians wonder why Paul handles his theological opponents so roughly in the letter. Would not love dictate a different procedure? Evidently Paul did not feel the situation called for gentle love. The gospel itself was being compromised and men's souls were in danger. What was needed was a pure testimony to the truth, not an ecumenical love-in. Paul warns us against a peace in the church without truth. Unity in the dark is not the unity the New Testament values. Paul was a man of great principle. He did not feel able to stand idly by while the gospel was compromised. He could see no value in seeking to coexist with error such as this. It was a time for great plainness of speech, and that is what Galatians is. We in the twentieth century church have much to learn from Paul along these lines.

The central chapters of the letter expound the nature of salvation. In them Paul develops an impressive theology of the Old Testament in order to display its Biblical roots. It seems that the false teachers had been urging the Galatian believers to accept circumcision and other observances of the Jewish law in order to secure salvation. Circumcision hardly seems like an issue with parallels in our day. But when we see that it stands as a symbol for the religion of legalism, the point becomes clearer. The Galatians were being led to suppose that faith in Christ did not secure right standing with God. It was necessary to augment the merit of Christ, on which Paul had taught them to trust, with human works. Therefore, Paul endeavors to show them how salvation is a free gift bestowed on believers on account of Christ's atonement. To that basis we can contribute precisely nothing. "A man is not justified by works of the law but through faith in Jesus Christ" (2:16). Anything else would make Christ to have died in vain (2:21).

Even in our day people are asking what is the real essence of the Christian message. It does not have to do with the dead formalism of external rules. This is what has turned so many off organized religion. Christianity is personal faith in Jesus and a living, continuing relationship with Him. And it all becomes ours by believing, not achieving. Christ took our place on the cross. He became a "curse" for us (3:13). Simply by trusting in Him and accepting His finished work on the cross, we are justified in God's sight. Saved existence does not take place in atomistic isolation, however. For those united to Christ by faith belong to the people of God and have become heirs of the promise given to Abraham (3:25-29). They are part of a new community based on grace and mercy, in which all that divides men in a fallen world can no longer divide them.

In the final two chapters, Paul discusses the matter of Christian holiness. We may be saved by faith alone, but saving faith is never alone. It is productive in the ethical realm. It would be a complete falsification of Paul's theology to charge that he was indifferent to how a person lived after he was converted. Justification means union with Christ, and that relationship has very definite moral implications for the concrete actions of believers. Christian freedom is freedom from sin, not freedom to sin.

In his development of this theme, Paul gives us some of his finest teachings on holiness and the Spirit filled life. A civil war is raging in every believer's experience. The only way he can find victory and bear fruit to God is to line up behind the Spirit and allow himself to be led by Him. In this manner spiritual fruit will appear in his life and ripen to maturity. In a day which features the new morality we can hardly question the extreme relevance of this teaching on holiness. We need to hear Paul's emphasis on the demands and responsibilities of the Christian life, and to be reminded of the resource from beyond ourselves, the Spirit, who is present in the midst of His people to fulfil in us the just requirement of the law.

Paul's Letter to the Galatians deals with questions of fundamental importance then and now. In each case the answer is Jesus Christ. How can we know the truth? Jesus Christ teaching us by speaking through His apostles. How can we find peace with God? Jesus Christ redeeming us through His cross. How can we walk the way of Christian holiness? Jesus Christ sanctifying us through His Spirit. This is "mere Christianity." Galatians has put the gospel in a nutshell. It has as much relevance to Christians in the twentieth century as it had in the first. It is the charter of Christian liberty. If we will heed its message we will not become enslaved to any kind of bondage again.

Galatians has not wanted for great expositors. This commentary makes no claim to great originality. And yet there is value simply in thinking through once again the teaching of so germinal a book as this. Galatians has launched spiritual revolutions in the past; it could do that again! The aim will be to concentrate on the great theological principles Paul sets forth, and to see how they could be applied to the situations we face today. May the Spirit who once gave this letter to be written perform a sanctifying work in all that read this book.

contents

Chapter One

the heart of the matter

Paul an apostle—not from men nor through man, but through Jesus Christ and God the Father, who raised him from the dead—and all the brethren who are with me, To the churches of Galatia: Grace to you and peace from God the Father and our Lord Jesus Christ, who gave himself for our sins to deliver us from the present evil age, according to the will of our God and Father; to whom be the glory for ever and ever. Amen. Galatians 1:1-5

Paul is the sender of this letter. The bare name was enough to introduce himself to the Galatians who knew him well. One of the least doubted facts in Biblical criticism has been the Pauline authorship of this letter. It breathes Paul's spirit and theology, and fits exactly into primitive Christian history as we know it. Reading the epistle carefully enables us to learn a surprising amount about the writer. Formerly he had been an ardent disciple of Judaism who believed persecuting the Christian church was the thing God wanted him to do. Out of this life-style Jesus Christ liberated him and set him apart for a life of missionary service. The very writing of this letter was in partial fulfilment of his commission. Christ had given him a message divine in origin, and it was a matter of supreme importance that its integrity be preserved. Paul was a man of great principle who could not stand by and let the truth of his message be compromised. The epistle reveals the depth of Paul's religious experience. He knew himself to be the bondslave of Jesus Christ. The reality of his walk with Christ and his experience of His grace shines through with great clarity.

Just in case we would think of Paul as a man in a class all by himself, there are also many details in the letter which reveal his humanity to us. He is shocked and hurt at the speedy defection of his converts from the purity of the gospel. He even wonders to himself whether his whole work among them might not prove to have been a failure. He can only describe his agony over the matter of their Christian growth in terms of a mother in the pains of childbirth. He admits to being perplexed over their behavior. In relation to the false teachers he is quite indignant. He is quite certain what the issues are and utters a divine curse on any who dare to preach another gospel. He did not even hesitate to rebuke Peter when the apostle behaved in a manner inconsistent with the gospel of grace.

From the introductory paragraph it is evident that Paul's authority and message have been called into question. In response Paul sets forth his authority as an apostle of Jesus Christ, and characterizes the Christian message as a gospel of divine grace. First, Paul speaks of himself as an apostle of Jesus Christ. This term was familiar to the Jewish mind. It refers to a special emissary who is sent out with legal authority to act on behalf of the one who commissioned him. It was the term Jesus used to describe the status and function of certain of His disciples. "He called his disciples, and chose from them twelve, whom he named apostles" (Luke 6:13). The apostles were men personally selected by Jesus Christ and authorized to speak and act in His name. To this select group Paul claims to belong on the basis of his appointment to that office by the risen Lord Himself. Paul wishes the reader to know at the outset that he is a personal representative of Jesus and speaks with His authority.

His apostleship, he wants us to know, came "not from men nor through man, but through Jesus Christ and God the Father." Paul's commission to Damascus had been authorized by the Jewish hierarchy in Jerusalem (Acts 9:2). But his apostolic commission had neither human source nor human agency. He was not elected to that office by a group of "men," nor did he come to it through the graces of some intermediary. It was to the risen Christ alone that he traced his calling, not to any human appointment.

Paul puts Christ alongside "God the Father, who raised him from the dead." Belief in the resurrection is central to the Christian faith. It is the supreme proof of the truth which Jesus proclaimed about Himself and the kingdom of God. This is the event by which God authenticated Jesus' credentials. Christianity could not have grown—and cannot survive—without it. It is important that we remember in a day which asks for reasons why, to believe that the gospel rests securely on the mighty acts of God in the midst of world history. The gospel does not depend merely on subjective religious experience. It is firmly rooted in this-worldly reality and can be checked out for its truth value.

In defending his apostleship, Paul's concern is not for any injured pride he might have after being attacked by the false teachers. His motives are not self-centered. He knew that those who sought to undermine his authority really had in mind perverting the gospel of grace. His attempt to defend his own apostleship is entirely motivated by a deep concern for the gospel. His person and his message were tied in together. The reason he defended his office was that he might defend Christ's gospel.

How well based was Paul's claim to be a true apostle? Was it on the order of Mormon Joseph Smith, who claimed to be an apostle on the flimsiest of grounds? The Galatian epistle shows that Paul's claim has solid foundation. The Jerusalem apostles, the original disciples of our Lord, were fully acquainted with Paul's claim and its basis, and they gladly extended to him the right hand of fellowship (2:9). They were convinced Paul was a true apostle. The entire Book of Acts is a powerful testimony to the validity of Paul's apostleship. It shows how the Spirit, first through Peter's and then through Paul's leadership, brought about the spread of the Christian movement throughout the Roman Empire. It is quite possible that the Galatians themselves had seen "the signs of an apostle" in Paul's miracle-working activity (3:5; cf. II Cor. 12:12).

Paul is not alone in his appeal to the Galatians. "All the brethren who are with me" join in the salutation. Evidently Paul had a circle of associates who traveled with him on his missionary journeys. No doubt they helped him extend the evangelistic outreach, instruct new converts, and care for the churches. In mentioning them, Paul may wish to show the Galatians that he does not stand alone in opposition to the Judaizing heresy that had crept into their churches. Many other Christians are deeply concerned about the same thing.

Here we find the clue to the nature of authority in Biblical religion. Our lives are to be subject to Jesus Christ speaking through His apostles. Although Paul is a believer in Christ as we are, we are not apostles as he is. Proper authority is vested, not in human consensus, but in apostolic teaching. The church is built on the foundation of the apostles and prophets. What is the reason for this? It is because salvation history has entered its definitive and final stage in Jesus Christ. All our thinking henceforth must be referred back to this normative beginning, which will not be succeeded or surpassed. The teachings of Christ and the apostles are therefore completely normative for the faith of all later Christians. All human opinion and tradition are to be measured and subordinated to this standard.

Theology in our day needs to hear this note. Many theologians like to place the opinions of modern man on the same level of authority with or even above apostolic doctrine. They regard the apostles as little more than first century believers whose opinions are not qualitatively better than their own. In this way they arrogate to themselves the authority that properly belongs to the apostolic witness. This was in effect just what the Galatians were being asked to do by the false teachers. But neither they nor we have any right to do so. The apostles of our Lord were unique and their word was to be binding. Of them Jesus said, "he who receives any one whom I send receives me; and he who receives me receives him who sent me" (John 13:20). We are to receive Paul's word as Christ's own. We are not to claim an authority on a level with that of Paul nor exalt our opinions over his teachings.

The same mistake can be made in regard to churchly tradition. Obviously we ought to have great respect for the history of Christian thought and the lessons men have learned over the centuries of walking with God. Indeed if we ignore our own history, we will in all probability have to repeat its mistakes. The gospel has been thought about for two thousand years now. To ignore that fact would be both uneconomical and an insult to the Spirit who has been working in the midst of His people all this time. Nevertheless, Scripture as the primal witness to the Christ event enjoys priority over tradition. Scripture is the critical standard by which tradition is to be measured. The church is the "minister" of the Word; she is not its "master." The opinions of the church corporate—no more than those of individual men—are not to be placed above apostolic teaching. Jesus specifically warned against equating tradition and the Word of God (Mark 7:8). In accepting the canon of Scripture, the church was pledging itself to hear it and obey it like nothing else. Paul does not write as one commissioned by the church, whether in Jerusalem or Rome. He writes as the personal representative of Jesus Christ. His authority was not human or ecclesiastical, it was divine. Therefore, we ought to submit to it.

Now Paul greets them and turns to the message he is charged with proclaiming. "Grace to you and peace from God the Father and our Lord Jesus Christ." The two nouns "grace" and "peace" are not carelessly set down. For they express with eloquence what the gospel is about. The grace of God is the reason we have any good news at all, and the nature of salvation is peace with God and peace within. Spiritual well-being springs from a right relationship with God in Christ.

Again we notice how God the Father and the Lord Jesus are coordinated. Together they are the dual source of divine blessing. The title "Lord" is one chosen by the Greek translators of the Hebrew Bible to stand for the divine name in the original. It is Paul's way of confessing the divine person of Jesus Christ, who is "God over all, blessed for ever" (Rom. 9:5). It is said that the doctrine of justification dominates the Epistle to the Galatians. But that is not altogether true. Paul is really more interested in the one who justifies sinners than in the benefit itself. Christ is central in the theology and faith of Paul. He dominates this letter. From the time that Paul met Him on the road to Damascus Paul's life was oriented and focused on Him. He was aware of Christ living within him (2:20). Christ crucified was the central theme of his preaching (3:1). The cross of Christ was all he cared to boast in (6:14). Everything that is ours in salvation comes to us in Christ (3:14, 26). No wonder he says elsewhere, "For to me to live is Christ, and to die is gain" (Phil. 1:21).

Having mentioned grace and peace, Paul turns to the saving event in which grace was exhibited and peace made available. He has already identified God the Father as the one who raised Christ from the dead. Now he refers to Christ as the one "who gave himself for our sins to deliver us from the present evil age." This is an important statement about the motive of the incarnation and the meaning of the cross. Jesus gave Himself up to death in a voluntary, sacrificial act. As the servant of the Lord, He has borne our griefs and carried our sorrows (Isa. 53:4). Paul focuses on Christ's death on Calvary, not His birth at Bethlehem. He understands the death of Christ, not as a display of love or an act of heroism, but as a redemptive sacrifice. Jesus gave up His life of His own accord (John 10:18) in order to put away our sins (Heb. 9:26). If only the Galatians could see that. To comprehend that Christ died for our sins is to recognize that we cannot save ourselves but must place our confidence in Jesus Christ.

The object of Christ's atoning death was to deliver us. Paul uses a strong verb which suggests a rescue from the power of another. It is used of God rescuing Joseph from his afflictions and the angel rescuing Peter from prison (Acts 7:10; 12:11). Salvation *is* a rescue operation! Often we think of the atonement and salvation in too exclusively legal terms.

It is important to remember also that the cross represents Christ's victory over the powers of darkness. At the cross Christ defeated the cosmic powers and pacified all opposition. Satan can no longer accuse us. The prince of this world has been cast out. Jesus Christ is Lord. In particular we have been rescued from "this present evil age." The distinction between "the present age" and "the age to come" was familiar to every Jew. Because of the Fall, the present age is under the power of the evil one (I John 5:19). What Christ has done is to transfer the believer from the sphere of Satan's power into a new order in which the life of the age to come can already be entered into. While still living here below he can enjoy provisionally the life of that new age. But because our roots go down deep in the soil of this present age, a powerful liberation is required to wrench them out and transplant them into fresh ground. Yet this is the very thing which Christ by His death has made possible.

Christ's decision to die for sins, Paul points out, was entirely in accord with "the will of our God and Father." The atonement was not the unaided activity of God the Son. It was the determined will of the Godhead to provide an atonement for sin. God Himself is the author of redemption. His mercy lies back of it all. Jesus Christ is "the lamb slain from the foundation of the world" (I Peter 1:18). We must avoid any suggestion of an antithesis between Jesus and God the Father. The action of the Son was proof of the Father's love. "He loved us and sent his Son to be the expiation for our sins" (I John 4:10). In the cross the will of Father and Son are in complete accord. What a rich statement on the nature of the atonement this is. We learn that the *nature* of Christ's death is sacrificial, that its *object* is man's deliverance, and that its *origin* is the eternal will of the triune God.

Already at this early point in the letter, Paul has introduced us to his major themes. The gospel must not be tampered with because it is Christ's, not Paul's. Christ is also the center of the message. There is good news because Christ died in the sinner's place. We see three steps in the theology of this introduction. God has provided objective salvation for mankind in the finished work of Christ. He is announcing the gospel through His apostolic messengers. The subjective benefits of salvation He freely offers to bestow on those who trust Christ. Is it any surprise that Paul closes with a doxology? "To whom be the glory for ever and ever. Amen." The only appropriate response to such grace is praise and thankful worship. Paul does not generally employ a doxology in the opening sentences of his letters. But as he considers what great things God has done for His people, his heart is filled with thanksgiving. For in the last analysis the issue at stake in his controversy with the Galatians is the glory of God. By their insistence on human achievement, the false teachers were downgrading and minimizing what God had done. By pointing to the all-sufficiency of Christ and His finished work, Paul was magnifying God's grace.

Chapter Two

authority in religion

I am astonished that you are so quickly deserting him who called you in the grace of Christ and turning to a different gospel—not that there is another gospel, but there are some who trouble you and want to pervert the gospel of Christ. But even if we, or an angel from heaven, should preace to you a gospel contrary to that which we preached to you, let him be accursed. As we have said before, so now I say again, If any one is preaching to you a gospel contrary to that which you received, let him be accursed. Am I now seeking the favor of men, or of God? Or am I trying to please men? If I were still pleasing men, I should not be a servant of Christ. Galatians 1:6-10

Paul's concern for the integrity of the gospel is such that he simply brushes aside any word of commendation or praise for the Galatian churches. Even the problem ridden Corinthian congregation was greeted more warmly (I Cor. 1:4-9). Paul was too deeply moved for that. "I am astonished," he began. He was appalled at what his young converts were planning to do. They were in the process of defecting from God and the gospel. The verb "defect" is used of military revolt and makes a colorful metaphor. Used here in the present tense, it suggests a process of spiritual desertion taking place. The prospect of it sickened Paul's heart and moved him to intervene in the hopes of preventing it. And they were doing it "so soon" after their conversion. Even before the gospel had time to lose its freshness, they were looking around for something new. They had surrendered to false teaching without a struggle.

The full gravity of their decision is indicated by the fact that God Himself is the one being deserted. "You are so quickly deserting *him* who called you." It was not simply a case of exchanging one theological opinion for another. It was not some technical mistake concerning an abstract point of doctrine. They were in process of abandoning a personal, loving God who had called them to salvation by His grace. The Galatians themselves certainly did not see it that way. No doubt they believed it was God leading them to a higher plateau of Christian experience. But Paul told it like it was! Had not he himself once sought to destroy the church, believing he was doing God a service? He was aware of the danger of putting religious feelings above the revealed truth of God. However sincere they were, the Galatians were wrong. Even their enthusiasm for God's law was mistaken and actually an act of rebellion against God. In a day like ours which places so much emphasis on existential experiences, it is especially important to measure our feelings by the objective truth of God's Word.

Paul regards the teaching of the Judaizers as "another gospel." It is not just the same message in a different dress. It is something of a different kind altogether. It does not even deserve the title "gospel." A theology that rests salvation on human achievement is not good news but bad. It leaves us without hope. When we consider that Paul is making this judgment of a message that was sound on the person of Christ, the vicarious atonement, the need for regeneration, and so forth (Paul does not suggest they denied any of these things), the point is even clearer. The gospel of Christ ought to be so precious to us that we cannot remain unmoved by its distortion in any important way.

The cause of all this trouble was a group of teachers set on creating turmoil in the congregation and distorting the truth of the gospel. By their teaching they were throwing the believers into a state of intellectual confusion. James uses the same verb when referring to these very people: "Since we have heard that some persons from us have *troubled* you with words, unsettling your minds, although *we gave them no instructions*" (Acts 15:24).

Evidently these false teachers represented the "right wing"

of Jewish Christianity and claimed to be representing James and the Jerusalem church. The claim was refuted by James at the Apostolic Council and by Paul in this epistle. These teachers not only unsettled the minds of believers, they also were set on willfully perverting the gospel. It was bad enough that the Galatians fell for their doctrinal trap. A little pity might be mixed with blame for them. But these teachers knew exactly what they were doing, and persisted in it. This makes their guilt the greater.

Perverting the gospel and troubling the people of God are related activities. Because the church lives by the gospel, the message cannot be changed without her existence being threatened. The result of this "other gospel" was the upsetting and unsettling of Christians. It brought doubt, confusion, and uncertainty because it struck right at the heart of the doctrine of salvation. Perhaps the greatest enemies of the church are not those who blatantly oppose the gospel, but those within her ranks who tamper with God's Word. They sap the church's vitality from within and make her vulnerable to all manner of spiritual diseases. Conversely, the way to nurture and build up the church is to believe and preach the gospel soundly.

Paul indicates just how serious the matter is by pronouncing a divine curse upon those guilty of perverting the gospel. He warns the Galatians to pay no attention to the outward qualifications of the teachers. Perhaps the Galatians had been overawed by these pretended messengers from the mother church in Jerusalem. Paul insists that they not receive another gospel, whoever brings it—even if it is an angel from heaven. Outward qualifications do not validate the message. The message validates the messenger. Any person who preaches another gospel is under the wrath of God and we ought to turn away from him in horror. Paul cannot understand why the Galatians have not done that, but instead actually welcomed what these teachers had to say. In case the Galatians have not yet grasped the point, Paul reiterates it. "If any one is preaching to you a gospel contrary to that which you received, let him be accursed." In this way he wants them to understand he is in dead earnest and not saying it in a rash fit of temper.

In this section we see Paul, the man of principle. We must not dismiss his language as an intemperate outburst, unworthy of the Spirit of Christ. It was a question of God's truth. Our Lord used language every bit as strong in denouncing religious teachers in His day who seemed bent on destroying God's truth and people. It is as a servant of Christ that Paul speaks here. As a man responsible to his Master, he feels compelled to speak plainly to the issues. His motives were completely pure. He was concerned for the honor of Christ whose gospel it was and for the souls of men that were at stake.

To teach that human works contribute to salvation is to say that Christ died for no purpose (2:21). It is to suggest that His work was insufficient and needed to be improved on. By teaching such things the Judaizers were obscuring the gospel, thus preventing sinners from hearing the only message that could save them. The real question this passage poses is not why Paul became so incensed by this error, but why we, confronted with even deeper error in our own day, seem not to be shocked or dismayed at all but accept it as a natural thing. It was the strong principles of men like Paul which built the Christian movement. Our easygoing tolerance is the sort of thing that could destroy it. Of those who cause believers to stumble, Jesus said, "It would be better for him if a great millstone were hung around his neck and he were thrown into the sea" (Mark 9:42).

The passage also teaches something about the nature of the gospel. It is a personal encounter with Christ in the context of objective truth. Its contents are not relative to the people who believe it. Becoming a Christian is to be "obedient from the heart to the standard of teaching to which you were committed" (Rom. 6:17). Anyone claiming to preach the gospel, whoever he may be, must conform his word to the authentic message of the apostles. We should not be overly impressed with personalities, whether of high ecclesiastical office or of great theological brilliance. The gospel is Christ's immutable message and its purity must be protected. Paul's astonishment was mixed with indignation. In turning away from the true gospel, the Galatians were incurring, not Paul's disappointment, but the strong displeasure of Jesus Christ Himself. If they were to continue on that route, they would be excluded from the very presence of God. Paul repeats himself because the matter is that solemn.

The lesson Paul is teaching is one we need to learn today.

Most of the leading theologians feel perfectly free to modify elements of the apostolic message to suit their taste. Many of them regard Biblical teaching as an altogether human set of religious symbols which elucidate the depths of experience enjoyed by those believing writers, but little more. They do not feel obligated to subject their thought to the normative truth of the apostolic gospel. They do not think it the norm and criterion by which all things should be tested.

Their attitude is evidently the same as that of the false teachers of Galatia. Paul's anathema rightly falls on anyone who teaches a message contrary to the primitive gospel. Let us not be dazzled by the dignity or scholarship of those who reject the gospel in our day. Teachers should be judged by the gospel, not the gospel by them. We need to test what we hear by the plain teaching of the New Testament. If it fails to pass the test we ought to reject it. If it accords with the word of the apostles we should embrace it and hold it fast.

> *For I would have you know, brethren, that the gospel which was preached by me is not man's gospel. For I did not receive it from man, nor was I taught it, but it came through a revelation of Jesus Christ. For you have heard of my former life in Judaism, how I persecuted the church of God violently and tried to destroy it; and I advanced in Judaism beyond many of my own age among my people, so extremely zealous was I for the traditions of my fathers. But when he who had set me apart before I was born, and had called me through his grace, was pleased to reveal his Son to me, in order that I might preach him among the Gentiles, I did not confer with flesh and blood, nor did I go up to Jerusalem to those who were apostles before me, but I went away into Arabia; and again I returned to Damascus.*
>
> *Then after three years I went up to Jerusalem to visit Cephas, and remained with him fifteen days. But I saw none of the other apostles except James the Lord's brother. (In what I am writing to you, before God, I do not lie!) Then I went into the regions of Syria and Cilicia. And I was still not known by sight to the churches of Christ in Judea;*

*they only heard it said, "He who once persecuted
us is now preaching the faith he once tried to
destroy." And they glorified God because of me.*
Galatians 1:11-24

Having gotten that off his chest, Paul now begins to
develop a historical argument in order to prove that he
received his gospel from Christ and not from men. He addresses the Galatians as his brethren, indicating that while he
criticizes their doctrine he loves them personally and still
thinks them to be Christians. He is aware of the charge
circulating from the false teachers that he was dependent for
his message and ministry on the Jerusalem church. It was
necessary to replace the fables with the facts. "I certify"—a
declaration of unusual solemnity—"that the gospel which was
preached by me was not man's gospel." He did not receive it
in the way in which Jewish beliefs and practices were handed
down. It was not something learned at school by rote and
repetition under the instruction of notable teachers. And it
certainly was not the invention of his own religious genius.
"It came through a revelation of Jesus Christ." He was not
educated into the kingdom of God. On the Damascus road
God unveiled for him what was previously hidden and secret.
At last Paul saw the true significance of Jesus, that He was
the Messiah of Old Testament promise.

Reared as he was in Jerusalem (Acts 22:3), Paul could not
help but be aware of the basic facts of Jesus' life. In persecuting the church, he must also have known what inter-
pretation Christians placed upon those facts. Nevertheless,
the bare knowledge of these things was not enough. He had
as yet no supernatural acquaintance with Jesus Christ. The
gospel had not yet been authenticated as true in his experience. God gave to him a transforming revelation. The content
of it was Jesus as the anointed of God. As he would later put
it, "When a man turns to the Lord the veil is removed" (II
Cor. 3:16). Early in the chapter Paul had asserted the divine
origin of his apostolic commission; here he asserts the divine
origin of his apostolic gospel. Neither his mission nor his
message derived from human sources. Both came from Jesus
Christ and God the Father.

In support of this bold claim, Paul alludes to his own life
situation just before, during, and after his conversion. Before

his conversion Paul was not in the least disposed to believe the Christian message. He had been a fanatical adherent of the Jewish religion and aggressively bigoted toward Christians. Religion in his case did not bring him nearer the truth. It kept him from finding it. He was at that time no likely candidate for conversion. He was infuriated by what he regarded as blasphemy and violently opposed the cause of Jesus. He outstripped many of his contemporaries in his complete devotion to the Jewish religion.

It is common in our day to interpret other religions as preparing people for the full divine revelation in Christ. But that is not always the case. The religious people in the Gospels were the ones furthest from the kingdom. Their religion was a cloak for great hardness of heart. Of course we want to believe that the Spirit is drawing the world to Christ in all kinds of ways unknown to us. Yet at the same time we ought not to idealize the value of religions. Religion kept Paul from Christ.

In view of his former life in Judaism, the glorious conversion Paul experienced can be attributed only to the powerful grace of God. God acted to save him. Paul had been bent on destroying the church when God broke in and changed his entire life. Part of the testimony of every believer is thanksgiving for the grace of God that went before and quickened in him just as the right moment a desire for the things of God. God never ceases to seek us out despite all our sinful efforts to evade His love. He is one from whom literally nothing can separate us except our refusal of His grace. God's calling is not irresistible. A man must respond to it. Later Paul would tell Agrippa, "I did not disobey the heavenly vision" (Acts 26:19).

God's promises are all conditional upon man's response. What God did was to reveal His Son in Paul. The wording is ambiguous, but the meaning must be *to* him and *through* him. What at first was a revelation to Paul was shortly to become a revelation through him to the Gentiles. That in itself is amazing. Before his conversion, Paul had thought the Gentiles unclean and outside God's saving purpose. Christ took that prejudice away, and the Galatians themselves were examples of the converts which resulted from Paul's obedience to his missionary calling.

Immediately after his dramatic conversion Paul felt more the need of quiet than of advice. Therefore, he did not consult either with the Christians in Damascus or with the apostles in Jerusalem. Instead he withdrew from public scrutiny into the region around Damascus where he could think through past experiences and concepts in the light of the new revelation. Paul does not tell us this out of pride. He did not despise the advice other Christians might have been able to give him. It was simply a matter of fact, a fact which refuted any charge that he was inferior to some teacher under whom he had been required to study. There was at this time no link between him and the Jerusalem church. What Paul did in "Arabia" is a matter for conjecture. No doubt it was a time of reflection on the messiahship of Jesus and what that meant for a child of the Old Testament.

After three years Paul did make the trip to Jerusalem. He was able to see Cephas and James over a period of fifteen days. His purpose in going up was to get to know Peter. It was not to seek out an "audience" with the "prince of the apostles." He simply wished to become acquainted with an esteemed apostle, one who was in an ideal position to fill him in on innumerable details about Jesus' life and the early growth of the church. It probably had the aspect of an interview, with Paul eager to learn whatever he could of the historical origins of the faith.

Any idea that Paul went there to get their approval for his ministry for which he was now indebted is ruled out. The visit was brief and fraternal. He did not go to be taught by the apostles, but to get acquainted with them. In fact, Peter was the only apostle he was to see. The reason for this could have been the fear of the other disciples. "When Paul came to Jerusalem he attempted to join the disciples; and they were all afraid of him, for they did not believe that he was a disciple" (Acts 9:26). They had not forgotten his persecuting activities of only a few years ago, and they probably suspected another trick. Were it not for Barnabas, perhaps he would not have met any apostles at all!

Following that brief visit there was no contact at all for a long time. Paul moved out into missionary activity in the northern regions of Palestine, which put him well out of range of Jerusalem's jurisdiction. It could not be said that he worked under their auspices. He was completely independent of Jewish-Christian sponsorship. The Christians in Judea knew about him, but did not know him personally. They kept receiving reports about his missionary successes, and this made them glad. They were thankful to God that the one who formerly had persecuted them so savagely had been converted and was now actively engaged in preaching the gospel. They glorified God because of Paul. This is important to Paul's argument, because it shows that his relations with these Jewish Christians were cordial. They accepted Paul completely and regarded him as a colaborer in the gospel. How different was the hostility Paul encountered from the Judaizers operating in the Galatian churches. Paul never had trouble with the Christians in Judea. The trouble arose from a small group pretending to represent Jewish Christianity but who in fact were distorting the position of the believers there.

Paul has made his point clear. His message came from the risen Lord. The fanaticism of his early life, his dramatic conversion, his independence from the Jerusalem church—all these conspire to prove that point. Having established it, Paul can appeal to the Galatian believers to obey God rather than men. Which detail of the Christian message is questioned will vary from age to age. The principle remains the same. Authority in religion rests with Jesus Christ and His apostles. If we cannot accept the gospel because of its superior truth, we ought to accept it because of its superior authority. The authority the Judaizers claimed was ecclesiastical; they claimed to be speaking for the Jerusalem church. Paul insists on the other hand that his mission and message did not come from any church but from Jesus Christ Himself. The Galatians should recognize his apostolic authority and accept it. They had done so on his first visit to them. They received him "as an angel of God, as Christ Jesus" (4:14). Now that his authority is being questioned and his message disputed, he expects them to recognize his authority still.

In a day of theological confusion such as ours, when we are deafened by a babel of voices, we should heed Paul's advice. Matters of belief ought to be tested by the teachings of the apostles of Jesus Christ. This is the kind of apostolic succession we can accept. The church is apostolic when it orients its life and thought to apostolic doctrine. This teaching, now permanently preserved in the New Testament, is to regulate the beliefs and practices of the church in every generation.

Chapter Three

justification by faith

Then after fourteen years I went up again to Jerusalem with Barnabas, taking Titus along with me. I went up by revelation; and I laid before them (but privately before those who were of repute) the gospel which I preach among the Gentiles, lest somehow I should be running or had run in vain. But even Titus, who was with me, was not compelled to be circumcised, though he was a Greek. But because of false brethren secretly brought in, who slipped in to spy out our freedom which we have in Christ Jesus, that they might bring us into bondage—to them we did not yield submission even for a moment, that the truth of the gospel might be preserved for you. And from those who were reputed to be something (what they were makes no difference to me; God shows no partiality)—those, I say, who were of repute added nothing to me; but on the contrary, when they saw that I had been entrusted with the gospel to the uncircumcised, just as Peter had been entrusted with the gospel to the circumcised (for he who worked through Peter for the mission to the circumcised worked through me also for the Gentiles), and when they perceived the grace that was given to me, James and Cephas and John, who were reputed to be pillars, gave to me and Barnabas the right hand of fellowship, that we should go to the Gentiles and they to the circumcised; only they would have us remember the poor, which very thing I was eager to do. Galatians 2:1-10

In this the first of two dramatic episodes in Paul's relationship with the leaders at Jerusalem, the principles on which the epistle turns begin to unfold. Both incidents rivet our attention on the evangelical truth of justification by faith and advance Paul's narrative to an important doctrinal statement of it. The crucial character of this concept for the nature of salvation and the concept of preaching cannot be over-emphasized.

After fourteen years Paul made another visit to Jerusalem. He had already been engaged in the Gentile mission for some time and his theology must have been well thought out. Why did he go to Jerusalem at this time? The Judaizers would be quick to pounce on this and make it look as if he went there out of obedience to the authority of the mother church. Paul says he went up "by revelation." He does not say how this revelation came. It might have come through a Christian prophet like Agabus (Acts 11:28) or in some other way. At any rate, the visit afforded him the opportunity to share with the leaders at Jerusalem just exactly what he was preaching on his missionary tours. The visit seems to have been private conversations with the apostles and elders rather than a general meeting of all believers. Paul knew that the stakes were very high. The outcome would determine whether his ministry had been in vain or not.

Taking Titus, a Gentile convert, along with him was a bold stroke. Paul wanted to be sure not only his message was accepted, but the fruits of it as well. Would they accept Titus as a Christian brother without reservation? This was the issue at the practical level. Paul's move immediately smoked out the opposition. It came in the form of "false brethren" who wormed their way into the meeting. The pressure group apparently did not represent apostolic opinion and their views were rejected, but it was a tense moment. No doubt these were the people who claimed later, "Unless you are circumcised according to the custom of Moses, you cannot be saved" (Acts 15:2). Having Titus along with him enabled Paul to clear this up at the practical level once and for all.

His daring move was vindicated. "Titus was not compelled to be circumcised." Paul successfully resisted this compromise of evangelical principles. He saw the motive of the pressure group as spying out the freedom we have in Christ. They were like intelligence agents moving furtively to build up a case against Paul on the basis of slackness toward Jewish ritual requirements. But as far as Paul was concerned, their real purpose was to subject his converts to the bondage of legalism. Accepting the Jewish law would be a return to slavery for them.

The issue was not trivial. Paul could make concessions to weak Christians, but not to false ones. Had he listened to the pressure group and allowed Titus to be circumcised, the truth of the gospel of grace would have been irreparably damaged. Paul is not fighting on his own behalf; he is eager to ensure that gospel truth will be upheld. God accepts sinners who trust in Christ for salvation. To reintroduce legal obligations and make our standing before God dependent on them is to surrender grace for a religion of human achievement.

Paul speaks of Peter, James, and John in a strange way: they are "those of repute" and "reputed to be pillars." What can be the explanation for this? We know he regarded them as bona fide apostles along with himself (1:17). But he had to choose his words carefully in the light of the Galatian situation. The false teachers had no doubt exaggerated the authority of the Jerusalem apostles in order to downplay Paul's. Indeed they did it to build up their own status as supposed emissaries of Jerusalem. Therefore, Paul adopts language that shows he respects the office of the apostles, but is not overawed by their persons. The extravagant claims made for them by the Judaizers were quite out of place.

Paul's conference at Jerusalem had a happy outcome. There was a mutual recognition of the authority and orthodoxy of both sides. Paul's message and mission were accepted as fully genuine by the Jerusalem leaders. Whatever differences there were, pertained to style of operations and not to doctrinal discrepancies. The episode completely refutes the charge of the false teachers of Galatia that Paul's authority was less than theirs and his message different from theirs. The Jerusalem apostles fully endorsed Paul's person and ministry. The gospel of grace was vindicated. As a fraternal gesture, motivated by real love, Paul agreed to do what he could to help the "poor." This is a reference to the saints in the Jerusalem church who were extremely destitute. None of Paul's Gentile churches were so poor. Later on Paul was able to raise a collection from them in fulfilment of his promise here.

From this incident we learn about the unity of the apostolic gospel. It is fashionable today to speak of the theologies of the New Testament—the Pauline, the Lukan, the Johannine, the Petrine. The implication is that these were different theologies with fundamental differences between them. This was not the case. The difference between Peter and Paul, for example, had to do only with the audiences they were called to reach in their two ministries. Reaching Jews certainly required a different style and emphasis than would be appropriate for reaching Corinthian pagans. But there is only one gospel for both groups. As Paul said elsewhere, "Whether then it was I or they, so we preached and so you believed" (I Cor. 15:11). Peter's preaching did not contradict Paul's: it complemented it. They had a different commission, but the same message.

> *But when Cephas came to Antioch I opposed him to his face, because he stood condemned. For before certain men came from James, he ate with the Gentiles; but when they came he drew back and separated himself, fearing the circumcision party. And with him the rest of the Jews acted insincerely, so that even Barnabas was carried away by their insincerity. But when I saw that they were not straightforward about the truth of the gospel, I said to Cephas before them all, "If you, though a Jew, live like a Gentile and not like a Jew, how can you compel the Gentiles to live like Jews?" We ourselves, who are Jews by birth and not Gentile sinners, yet who know that a man is not justified by works of the law but through faith in Jesus Christ, even we have believed in Christ Jesus, in order to be justified by faith in Christ, and not by works of the law, because by works of the law shall no one be justified.* Galatians 2:11-16

Paul's clash with Peter is revealing both of Paul's independence of other apostles and of the evangelical principle of justification by faith. It is quite a spectacle. Two of the greatest apostles locked in confrontation. Paul calls Peter to account for his conduct as a Christian leader.

It is not difficult to figure out what happened. Peter had

been in the habit of eating with Gentile Christians. In line with early Christian custom, the common meal would have included the Lord's Supper. Then a pressure group from Jerusalem arrived, claiming to have been sent by James. They may well have been from his circle (cf. Acts 15:24). But it is certain he did not send them to create dissension in the church at Antioch. At any rate their presence caused Peter to withdraw from the common table with Gentile believers. For this Paul stood up against him because he was clearly in the wrong. Though he respected him as a pillar apostle, he had to expose this act of duplicity.

Peter knew as well as Paul that God accepted Gentiles and Jews alike on the basis of Christ's death. His vision of the great sheet lowered, containing all kinds of clean and unclean animals, had taught him a never-to-be-forgotten lesson. "What God has cleansed, you must not call common" (Acts 10:9-16). So it was not that Peter did not know better. He simply did not have the courage of his convictions, and actions speak louder than words. What made matters worse was the great effect Peter's actions had on others. The rest of the Jews and even Barnabas went along with him. It was an emergency situation. A split in the church was imminent and the truth of the gospel was about to be lost.

As soon as Paul saw what was happening, he made it a matter of public attention. He could not keep quiet about this issue. A public scandal had to be publicly confronted. Leaders in the church were not living according to the spirit of the gospel. Peter had been living like a non-Jew. The reference here is to the complicated food laws which made social intercourse between Jews and Gentiles almost impossible. Yet by this action he was implying that Gentile believers were not quite as good as Jewish ones. They lacked something which the others had. This was the very point the false teachers in Galatia wanted to make. And Peter was playing into their hands.

There was clearly a principle at stake. Paul did not act in an outburst of temper or even jealousy. He saw that we must welcome all whom Christ has welcomed (cf. Rom. 15:7). If He accepts them by faith, we cannot reject them. The fact that the Lord's Supper was involved makes it all the more serious. It is the sacrament of the unity of the body of Christ (I Cor. 10:17). To refuse to eat the Supper with fellow believers is deeply schismatic. When our disunity affects fellowship at the Lord's table, it is a sin against the body which God by His Spirit has created.

Even great ministers of the gospel make serious mistakes. We should never idolize one of God's servants. It is important that our faith rest on God's Word and not on any fallible human authority. This incident stands as a warning against crediting any office, even the "Petrine office," with infallibility. From Peter's experience we learn that it is not enough to believe the gospel if we do not practice it. Peter's offense was in the area of behavior, not creed. Our evangelical principles need to be fleshed-out in concrete situations. It would have been easy for Peter to have said, "It was such a small thing to get worked up about." It may have seemed small, but its true significance was profound. It is an affront to God and destructive to the church when we are slow to accept all those whom God has already accepted in Christ. It is said that eleven o'clock Sunday morning is the most segregated hour of the week in America. Black and white believers meet separately to worship one God and Savior. It is a sin against the body and a sin against the Lord. We should have no peace about it until the situation is changed.

Truth is more important than peace. Peter thought his slight compromise would not be noticed but would put the "circumcision party" at ease. He was sure they would leave shortly, after which things would normalize. He did not realize that the disciples of Christ are called to obedience, not to compromise. How often we act as if we were situation ethicists, as if God's laws could be suspended for a moment while some tricky situation irons itself out. It is not so. We must oppose any and all who seek to water down the truth of the gospel or curtail its application in any way. Where are men today like Paul and Luther, who were prepared to stand for truth, whatever the cost to them personally?

> *But if, in our endeavor to be justified in Christ, we ourselves were found to be sinners, is Christ then an agent of sin? Certainly not! But if I build up again those things which I tore down, then I prove myself a transgressor. For I through the law died to the law, that I might live to God. I have been crucified with Christ; it is no longer I who live, but*

Christ who lives in me; and the life I now live in the flesh I live by faith in the Son of God, who loved me and gave himself for me. I do not nullify the grace of God; for if justification were through the law, then Christ died to no purpose. Galatians 2:17-21

What is the truth Peter "knows" and is in danger of allowing to slip? It is the doctrine of justification by faith. Salvation is the gift of God. It cannot be earned. "To one who does not work but trusts him who justifies the ungodly, his faith is reckoned as righteousness" (Rom. 4:5). Jewish theology at the time believed that justification would take place at the last judgment if one's good deeds outweighed the bad. For Paul, justification takes place now and on the basis of the finished work of Christ, not on our merits. He heaps phrase upon phrase in order to emphasize this truth. Sinners are accepted by God through simply trusting Jesus.

Is justification by faith something that speaks to modern man? Where are the points of contact between this doctrine and ordinary life? Our generation has its own way of asking Bildad's question of centuries ago: "How then can man be righteous before God?" (Job 25:4). One of the most universal human experiences is the feeling of culpability or guilt. We are conscious of loving ourselves more than we should. Our lives are so often broken and we wonder where we can find wholeness again. Primitive man expressed his malaise in religious acts like sacrifices. Secular man tries to shift his guilt by such techniques as psychoanalysis. It is the same awareness of something wrong and of innocency lost in each case. Where can we find unconditional love and acceptance? The Bible speaks in categories which are transcultural. Man's nature and needs remain fundamentally the same. It is good news to learn that God is gracious and willing to accept sinners who come to Him in His Son.

Does the doctrine of justification by faith weaken man's sense of moral responsibility? If God justifies bad people, what point is there in being good? Paul recoils from such blasphemy with horror. "God forbid!" If after justification I were to go on sinning, Christ could not be blamed. The fault would be entirely my own. But the question assumes that justification is extrinsic to man's moral life. It is not. We are justified into *union* with Christ. We do not remain the same old people we were before justification. The justified sinner enters into a vital relationship with Jesus Christ. We are justified *in Christ*. We have died and risen again. Christ lives in us. Paul uses a number of expressions to bring out this point.

Sons of the Reformation have often been guilty of an extrinsic view of justification—as though a man might be declared righteous in God's sight and go on living the way he did before. This is completely unscriptural.

Justifying faith must issue in concrete righteousness. Only those who do not understand this could suppose Paul and James are in contradiction on this point (cf. James 2:14-26). Believers do not enjoy the assurance of justification independent of their actual lives. The New Testament is full of warnings against presuming such a thing. Paul's teaching later in this epistle about sowing and reaping is addressed to Christian believers. "He who sows to his own flesh will from the flesh reap corruption" (6:8). The justified person is washed and sanctified at the same time (I Cor. 6:11). We must not allow the doctrine of justification to be separated from the doctrine of our union with Christ. "As therefore you received Christ Jesus the Lord, so live in him" (Col. 2:6). Romans 5 is followed by Romans 6. It is not just a matter of feeling. Doesn't gratitude make you want to live like a Christian? It is a matter of theological fact. The Christ who was for us is the Christ who is in us. Christ the Savior is Christ the Lord. It cannot be any other way.

This is an admission of considerable ecumenical importance. How big is the gap between the Reformation and Rome now? If the Reformation is stressing a declaring just that implies a making just, and Rome emphasizes a making just that implies a declaring just, what is all the fuss about? Is it not time we sat down together again and found out where matters stood? The New Testament regards divisions in the church a very serious matter indeed. If we continue divided merely out of habit and not because of deeply felt principles, surely we deserve the judgment of God.

In a closing remark, Paul connects grace and the death of Christ. If we can justify ourselves, we nullify grace and declare the cross of Christ to have been redundant. This is the true character of works-religion. It robs Christ of His glory and negates the free grace of God. Paul, for his part, will have none of this. The twin hinge on which the Christian religion turns is the grace of God and the death of Christ. Anyone who claims he can earn salvation by his own efforts is undermining the foundation of the gospel. Grace and atonement count for nothing if we are the masters of our destiny and can save ourselves.

> *O foolish Galatians! Who has bewitched you, before whose eyes Jesus Christ was publicly portrayed as crucified? Let me ask you only this: Did you receive the Spirit by works of the law, or by hearing with faith? Are you so foolish? Having begun with the Spirit, are you now ending with the flesh? Did you experience so many things in vain?—if it really is in vain. Does he who supplies the Spirit to you and works miracles among you do so by the works of the law, or by hearing with faith?* Galatians 3:1-5

The point made, the epistle could have stopped here. But Paul turns once again to the Galatians themselves. He hopes he can bring them to their senses by an appeal to their own spiritual experience. He feels they have been plain foolish. He will not have them shift the blame to someone else. They should have known better. It is not so much their treachery as their folly which strikes Paul. It was as if a witch had cast a magic spell over them. Before their very eyes Christ had been displayed as crucified. This must refer to the content of Paul's preaching when he established the Galatian churches. He could tell the Corinthians: "For I decided to know nothing among you except Jesus Christ and him crucified" (I Cor. 2:2). Paul's theology was dominated by the cross. He dwelled constantly on the fact and significance of it. It was his only boast (6:14). In the light of this, Paul puts a simple question to them. He seems to be asking for information. But it is really a teaching device. Both he and they know the answer already. But they seem to be dull pupils and need to have the answer drawn out of them.

He suggests that the Galatians reflect for a moment on their own spiritual experience. How did their Christian life begin? The Spirit did not come on them because they were

morally good. He came as they heard the gospel and believed
it. And if they began on the supernatural level, what sense
does it make to drop back down to a religion of works? The
questions are rhetorical; the answers are obvious. One cannot
be a Christian without knowing that salvation is a free gift of
God. Spirit and flesh stand for two religions. We are saved by
God's grace, not our achievement. To go back to legalism as
the Galatians were proposing to do was spiritual desertion
and the height of folly. Surely all that they experienced of
the Spirit and His gifts was not in vain. To taste of Christian
freedom and then to go back to the law is sheer lunacy.

We can be grateful for Paul's controversy with the Galatians, for it led him to develop his great doctrine of justification by faith. There are other ways in which we can speak of
salvation, such as dying and rising with Christ and the new
birth. But justification is unique in pointing to the triumph
of grace in the theology of Paul. God has acted in Jesus
Christ to save man. He pronounces us righteous and pardons
all our sins. And by means of this act He also gives us the
power to live according to righteousness. "For the law of the
Spirit of life in Christ Jesus has set me free from the law of
sin and death" (Rom. 8:2).

Chapter Four

a theology of the old testament

Thus Abraham "believed God, and it was reckoned to him as righteousness." So you see that it is men of faith who are the sons of Abraham. And the scripture, foreseeing that God would justify the Gentiles by faith, preached the gospel beforehand to Abraham, saying, "In you shall all the nations be blessed." So then, those who are men of faith are blessed with Abraham who had faith. Galatians 3:6-9

Having established his case by means of an argument from history and an appeal to the experience of the Galatians themselves, Paul proceeds to develop a theology of the Old Testament. He wishes to demonstrate how the doctrine of justification by faith originates and is deeply rooted in sacred Scripture. Salvation by grace through faith is a central theme, not only of the New Testament message, but of the Old Testament as well. This is a conviction that needs stressing even in our day. For there are many people, even students of the Bible, who entertain the opinion that Old Testament religion was a religion of law and not gospel. In the central section of the epistle Paul develops an impressive case that this is not so. The law of God was given within the covenant of grace and did not nullify that agreement based on faith one whit.

Paul begins his understanding of Scripture with the great patriarch Abraham. It was a master stroke. If the false teachers wanted to reach back to Moses, Paul could go back further to Abraham, the esteemed ancestor of the Israelites. He lived in a period prior to the law, the temple, and circumcision. Why, he was even a Gentile before God called him! What interests Paul about the patriarch is the response Abraham made to God's call. He took God at His word. He did not try to *do* anything. When the promise came to him, he simply *believed* it. This was the great distinctive which the Book of Genesis brings out about him. He did not win right standing with God by his own efforts; it was given to him as a result of his faith. He did not scoff at the offer because it was too easy. He accepted God's word at its face value. So God reckoned his faith as righteousness. Just exactly what the Galatians needed to hear! Salvation is by believing, not achieving.

The implication is obvious. Abraham's kin are those who, like him, are trusting God to do for them what they have given up trying to do for themselves. They bear His family likeness. Paul's conclusion resembles a judgment Jesus made regarding the Jews of His day. They claimed physical descendancy from Abraham but were most unlike him in their attitude to God (John 8:33-44). Those "of the faith party" (as the phrase could be rendered, v. 7) stand to inherit the Old Testament promises, not those of the "circumcision party" (2:12). Abraham's true descendants are those who, like him, trust God to save them.

Paul makes his point at greater length in Romans 4. Abraham was justified by faith (vv. 1-8). It was reckoned to him for righteousness before he received the sign of circumcision (vv. 9-11). That makes him the father of all those who follow his example (v. 12). Paul's thought should make us very wary of what is called dispensational theology, which posits two entirely separate purposes of God for Israel and the church. Obviously Paul does not accept any such dichotomy in the plan of salvation. He calls believers "sons of Abraham" without sensing any incongruity.

Then Paul appeals to Scripture for a further point. Not only was Abraham justified by faith, he is definitely linked to the Gentile peoples. "In you shall all the nations be blessed." In the calling of Abraham, God already had the salvation of the Gentiles in mind.

The manner in which Paul speaks of this truth is instructive. He refers to Scripture as "foreseeing" that God would justify the Gentiles by faith. It is not that he regards Scripture as itself a personal agent. Rather, so closely does he identify what Scripture says with what God says that it becomes possible to speak in this way. What Scripture says is the equivalent of what the divine author of Scripture says. This manner of speaking takes us to the heart of Paul's doctrine of inspiration. The Bible is the voice of God. What Scripture says, God says. Every promise it contains is a divine promise, by the very fact that it is Biblical. Scripture is a divine oracle, and possesses irrevocable and binding authority. The relevance of this fact for the religious and theological confusion of our time is very evident. Contemporary theology has become relativistic and hesitating because it has given up any standard by which to measure its concepts. It is definitely the time for those who accept Paul's high doctrine of inspiration to set it forth cogently as the answer to modern man's quest for religious certainty.

What did the Scripture "foresee"? It looked beyond the case of Abraham, whom God was at that moment justifying by faith, and anticipated a time when people of all the nations would enter into the same blessing. They would be blessed exactly as Abraham was, through a faith response to God's gracious invitation and calling. The truth of justification, which was anticipated so clearly long ago, has now become visible and available in the gospel of Jesus Christ. Indeed, as Paul concludes, men of faith are even now blessed along with Abraham. They are enjoying God's favor because they are believing God just as he did. Here we see the unity of the Bible. The only demand God makes of men in connection with salvation is the trusting attitude of faith. Had the Galatians only consulted Scripture for themselves they would not have fallen such easy prey to the false teachers.

> *For all who rely on works of the law are under a curse; for it is written, "Cursed be every one who does not abide by all things written in the book of the law, and do them." Now it is evident that no man is justified before God by the law; for "He who through faith is righteous shall live"; but the law does not rest on faith, for "He who does them shall live by them." Christ redeemed us from the curse of the law, having become a curse for us—for it is written, "Cursed be every one who hangs on a tree"—that in Christ Jesus the blessing of Abraham*

might come upon the Gentiles, that we might re-
ceive the promise of the Spirit through faith. Galatians 3:10-14

Paul can hear the objection to what he has said. "It's all
very well talking about Abraham who lived *before* the law
was given. The real point is that we live *after* it was given, and
are obliged to observe it to the letter. In Abraham's time
there was as yet no law to keep. What about the law? Speak
to the issue!"

In replying to the would-be lawkeepers, Paul turns the
tables on them. He places the two ways of approaching God
side by side, and contrasts the results. Unknown to the
Galatians, an appeal to the law as a means of salvation
backfires badly. It lands the person following a religion of
works under the divine curse. To prove it Paul cites a text
from Moses' speech to the people of Israel on Mount Ebal.
"Cursed be he who does not confirm the words of this law by
doing them" (Deut. 27:26). Failure to keep God's law will
incur divine judgment. If our standing before God depends
on our success in completely complying with all of God's
statutes, we could have no assurance of being saved at all.
Obviously the religion of works is a dead-end street.

Paul is not denying any function to the law. He is merely
denying that its function is a saving one. Paul's words about
God's curse strike our modern ears as harsh. We do not like
to think of God cursing anyone. The Bible, however, teaches
that disobedience exposes us to God's wrath. Sin against a
holy God cannot be done with impunity. The effect of God's
law taken alone is condemnation and death. It is not the path
to life.

The path to life Paul finds set forth in a text in the
prophets (Hab. 2:4). "He who through faith is righteous shall
live." This verse was a favorite of New Testament writers (cf.
Rom. 1:17; Heb. 10:38). It connects faith, righteousness, and
life, three great concepts of the gospel. The text is not used
so much to prove the doctrine of justification by faith as to
illustrate it. Paul has already proved it from the life of
Abraham. Yet all the germinal ideas are also present in the
Habakkuk passage. "Faith" becomes faith in Christ, "Righteous" means accounted righteous, and "live" refers to saved
existence. The law, in sharp contrast, rests on an entirely

different foundation. It calls on us, not to believe, but to achieve. "The law does not rest on faith" (v. 12). It does not relate to the matter of justification at all. All it does is to lay down principles of conduct. It can do nothing to help those who have failed to keep those principles.

Thanks to the grace of God, man's universal failure to live up to God's standards has been taken care of in the death of Jesus on the cross. "Christ redeemed us from the curse of the law." This single fact makes our lack of achievement unimportant. There is a new possibility altogether for sinners. To express himself Paul employs a commercial metaphor, that of "redemption." In the ancient world a ransom was the price paid for the purchase of a slave or the release of a prisoner of war. In the Old Testament it denoted the payment of a price (Exod. 30:12). Jesus referred to His own death as a ransom (Mark 10:45). Peter speaks of our being "ransomed with the precious blood of Christ" (I Peter 1:18 f.). Jesus by His death bought us out from under the curse which our failure to keep the law had incurred. His blood is the means of our release. As Paul writes elsewhere, "You were bought with a price" (I Cor. 6:20).

Paul does not leave the matter there. He goes on to tell us how it is that Christ's death is capable of redeeming us. His language is strong and his meaning unmistakable: "Having become a curse for us." Christ Himself bore the curse that was due us. He took our place and became our substitute. The thought is quite parallel with something else Paul penned: "For our sake he made him to be sin who knew no sin, so that in him we might become the righteousness of God" (II Cor. 5:21). Jesus Christ became an accursed thing for our sakes.

This idea does not come easily to modern minds. Modern theology prefers to leave the idea of atonement ambiguous, omitting the notion of substitution altogether. This we cannot possibly do if we would be faithful to Paul's teaching. According to his theology, man is under the curse because of his sin, and something had to be done about that fact. The divine solution was the death of Christ. By that act God reconciled the world to Himself. Christianity is a religion of redemption, a religion of what God has done for man.

One sharp line between evangelical and nonevangelical theology is the doctrine of the atonement. Evangelical theology understands the atonement in objective terms. The cross is God's answer to the question how a God both merciful and holy can make sinners His sons. How is it possible for Him to pardon sinners in a way consistent with His own nature? The New Testament sees the cross as the means appropriate to the free offer of His love. "In this is love, not that we loved God but that he loved us and sent his Son to be the expiation for our sins" (I John 4:10). God does not love us because Christ died for us; Christ died for us because God loves us. The cross is the divine provision for the justification of sinners. A theology that downplays the substitutionary atonement has the effect, not only of denying plain Biblical teaching, but also of casting lost man once again on his own resources. And these are totally inadequate to save him.

In this connection Paul quotes a text from Old Testament law: "A hanged man is cursed by God." Death by hanging was the outward sign in Israel of being under God's curse. Christ's crucifixion, therefore, vividly pointed to the curse He was in fact enduring. The very manner of His death contains theological truth. Even this was a fulfilment of Old Testament religion.

In the death of Christ God has brought to fulfilment the promise He made to Abraham: "that in Christ Jesus the blessings of Abraham might come upon the Gentiles, that we might receive the promise of the Spirit by faith" (v. 14). The benefits of Christ's death do not become the possession of any man automatically. They must be received by faith, in a living union with Jesus Christ. Paul mentions the gift of the Spirit in particular because it represents all the blessings believers receive and is the "earnest" of them (II Cor. 1:22). Jew and Gentile alike (Paul shifts to the pronoun "we") receive by faith the gift of the Spirit, the distinguishing mark of a child of God. The new people of God, made up of both groups, has come to inherit the blessings of the Old Testament promise.

In this section Paul has compared a religion of *do* with a religion of *done*. Trying to please God by a proud reliance on one's achievement leads only to condemnation and death. Trusting in what God has done in the death of Christ leads to blessing and salvation. Notice the solid theological content which lay beneath New Testament preaching. A proclamation full of content was made before an appeal was made to receive Christ. Much damage has been done in our day by those who called for decisions before they had informed people what they were deciding about. A meaningful decision for Christ requires the awareness of doctrinal truth.

> *To give a human example, brethren: no one annuls even a man's will, or adds to it, once it has been ratified. Now the promises were made to Abraham and to his offspring. It does not say, "And to offsprings," referring to many; but, referring to one, "And to your offspring," which is Christ. This is what I mean: the law, which came four hundred and thirty years afterward, does not annul a covenant previously ratified by God, so as to make the promise void. For if the inheritance is by the law, it is no longer by promise; but God gave it to Abraham by a promise.* Galatians 3:15-18

Now Paul addresses himself to the question of an imaginary opponent. Does not the law rescind the earlier promise given to Abraham? Did it not annul the earlier agreement? Is it not by law-keeping that God's blessings now must be received?

Paul begins by appealing, as was Jesus' custom, to a fact of common knowledge. In the case of a human will and testament, he argues, it is impossible to change it once it has been duly ratified. And, if this is true of human wills, how much more unalterable must God's testament be? Certainly, the agreement with Abraham cannot be cancelled.

Into this argument Paul inserts a short caveat about the significance of the singular collective term "offspring" or "seed." It is a kind of "extra" to his argument, and reflects rabbinic training. It may be that in his dialogue with the Judaizing false teachers, he finds it useful to employ a line of argument quite similar to their own style of reasoning. We know that Paul is not unaware that "offspring," while singular in form, is plural in meaning. Later in this very chapter, he refers to believers as Abraham's "seed" (v. 29). Rather, he finds it deeply appropriate that the singular is used. He sees a profound theological significance in that singular noun. The true fulfilment of the ancient promise to Abraham, in whom all the nations are to be blessed, is none other than Jesus

Christ Himself. In Him the promise is embodied and mediated.

Getting back to his main point, Paul observes that law came in a full four centuries after the promise was given. The promise has obvious priority over law, and law cannot annul it. That being the case, we cannot possibly speak of salvation by law. Scripture is not self-contradictory. If the law were given to save people, it would represent a basic change of God's dealing with man. But since the Old Testament is clear that salvation is a free gift bestowed on believers, the law cannot be interpreted in that way. Paul's argument is based on the unity of the Bible. Because God promised salvation to Abraham—and in him all nations—by grace through faith, law cannot be understood in a way that would contradict this truth. Paul rejects any theology that would speak of a "dispensation of law" by which is meant a period in which salvation was actually conditioned on obedience to law. Salvation is now, and always was, by grace through faith.

> *Why then the law? It was added because of transgressions, till the offspring should come to whom the promise had been made; and it was ordained by angels through an intermediary. Now an intermediary implies more than one; but God is one. Is the law then against the promises of God? Certainly not; for if a law had been given which could make alive, then righteousness would indeed be by the law. But the scripture consigned all things to sin, that what was promised to faith in Jesus Christ might be given to those who believe.* Galatians 3:19-22

Paul's answer to the previous question gives rise to another. If the promise was unaffected by the giving of the law, why was the law given at all? Would not this view suggest that law had no place at all in religion? Later on this question developed into a malicious rumor which circulated among the Jewish Christians in Jerusalem that Paul actually encouraged the diaspora Jews to "forsake Moses" (Acts 21:21). The rumor was based on a distortion of Paul's actual position. Here Paul tells us how he understands law, where it fits into God's plan, and what function it fulfils.

"It was added because of transgressions." The law was given to awaken man's awareness of his sins. Though it had no power to make him holy, it could arouse him to perceive the reality of his transgressions. As such it would create in man a desire for deliverance. It teaches us our moral bankruptcy so well that we long for God's grace and the fulfilment of His promise. The age of law served as a kind of interlude until Christ came to deliver those under the law and to preach deliverance to the captives.

Paul sees a further indication of the inferiority of the law in the fact that it was ordained by angels through an intermediary. Although the Old Testament says nothing about angels playing a role in the giving of the law, it was a rabbinic belief and the conviction of early Christian preachers (cf. Acts 7:58; Heb. 2:2). The intermediary referred to is Moses. Paul feels that all this points to the secondary character of law. Surely a promise given by direct divine revelation is superior to a law mediated through angels and men. His later teaching on the incarnation (4:4-7) amplifies and heightens the point about the directness of God's revelation of grace. In political life, more significance is attached to a treaty which the president himself negotiates in a summit conference, than to one worked out at the lower diplomatic level. In both cases the agreement is taken to be binding, but somehow a greater degree of importance is attached to the first. In law, God deals with us through a system of mediation, whereas in the gospel He deals with us directly, one to one.

At the same time, the law is not in any way against the promises of God (v. 21). Promise and law complement one another. Both were divinely given, but for two different purposes. Law was not given to convey life. Even when operating perfectly the law was limited to the exposing of sin. That was the function it was meant to perform, and it does it well. God knows what He is doing. He did not give the law to undo what He had earlier planned to do. Promise and law fit into one coherent divine plan. Life is offered to man always and only on the basis of God's love and grace. The law, like a jailor, has locked us all up in the prison house of sin. Or to put it more plainly, the law reveals the universality of sin and shows us how intractable our plight is. It tells us, "All have sinned and come short of the glory of God" (Rom. 3:23). The most it can do is to drive us to seek Christ, in whom there is forgiveness of sins and the promise of everlasting life.

The theology of the Old Testament is a coherent whole. The law does not annul God's promise given to Abraham because the law was not given to bestow salvation. Many people suppose the Bible to be a hopeless tangle of mutually contradictory concepts. It is not. If we will but give it patient study, we too will discover in Scripture a single, coherent story of God's gracious purpose throughout history.

> *Tell me, you who desire to be under law, do you not hear the law? For it is written that Abraham had two sons, one by a slave and one by a free woman. But the son of the slave was born according to the flesh, the son of the free woman through promise. Now this is an allegory: these women are two covenants. One is from Mount Sinai, bearing children for slavery; she is Hagar. Now Hagar is Mount Sinai in Arabia; she corresponds to the present Jerusalem, for she is in slavery with her children. But the Jerusalem above is free, and she is our mother. For it is written, "Rejoice, O barren one that dost not bear; break forth and shout, thou who art not in travail; for the desolate hath more children than she who hath a husband." Now we, brethren, like Isaac, are children of promise. But as at that time he who was born according to the flesh persecuted him who was born according to the Spirit, so it is now. But what does the scripture say? "Cast out the slave and her son; for the son of the slave shall not inherit with the son of the free woman." So, brethren, we are not children of the slave but of the free woman. For freedom Christ has set us free; stand fast therefore, and do not submit again to a yoke of slavery.* Galatians 4:21—5:1

Later in the epistle Paul draws extensively on the Old Testament to illustrate his point about divine grace and Christian freedom. He recounts the story of Isaac and Ishmael, and elicits some deep spiritual truths. It is not an allegory in the sense that the literal meaning is negated. What

Paul sees in the passage from Genesis is fully compatible with its original intention. The kind of exegesis we find here is thoroughly rabbinic. Paul reasoned that, if the Galatians had such an interest in things Jewish, they ought to be impressed by an argument in this style. It required no special effort on Paul's part since he had been trained in Biblical exegesis under Gamaliel. God was able to use a skill Paul had acquired before conversion for the preaching of the gospel.

The Galatians are enamored of the law, are they? Good: then let them listen to what it says. Again Paul appeals to Abraham rather than Moses, this time to the fact that he had two sons. This was legitimate because the law included not only moral and religious legislation but also the history of the saving acts of God which began with Abraham. Paul wants the Galatians to see just exactly what the law says to this present situation. The Jews were fond of claiming Abraham as their father. Paul wishes them to reflect on whom they claim as their mother. Although Isaac and Ishmael had the same father, they did not have the same mother. Paul finds great significance in these mothers and their children. Ishmael was born according to the normal run of events. There was nothing miraculous about his birth. It was a birth by natural means. Isaac, however, was born because of the effective promise of God, which does what it says. As Hebrews puts it: "By faith Sarah herself received power to conceive, even when she was past the age, since she considered him faithful who had promised" (11:11). Thus Ishmael was the result of Abraham's reliance on his human planning, while Isaac was the product of his trusting in the promise of God. Not only was Abraham saved by faith, but faith is the principle which his whole life expounds.

"Now this is an allegory." Paul begins to search out the spiritual meaning embedded in this familiar story. Beneath the literal meaning there is exemplified a great spiritual truth. The women and their sons stand for two covenants, or two kinds of religion. Ishmael represents Abraham's effort to earn God's blessing through his own efforts. Isaac represents a religion of divine grace. The two stand for unbelief and faith in Abraham's life. The Judaizers at Galatia are spiritually the children of the covenant characterized by works-righteousness, not the covenant made with Abraham. Trying to win salvation by keeping the law leads to hopeless bondage. The sons of this covenant are destined to be slaves. The Judaizers were no better spiritually than the "Ishmaelites" despised by the Jews. Hagar corresponds to present-day Jerusalem in that these unbelieving Jews wish to remain at Mount Sinai rather than enter into the promised land.

Sarah, on the other hand, corresponds to the true people of God who trust in God to save them. What is the "Jerusalem above" to which Paul makes reference? The Bible is a book of eschatological hope. Many of its prophecies relate to a Jerusalem which is to come (Isa. 2:2-4, etc.). This city of the future was in sharp contrast with the miserable Jerusalem of the present. The Jerusalem above refers to the ideal city which God will bring into history in His own time. John the Seer spoke of it: "I saw the holy city, new Jerusalem, coming down out of heaven from God, prepared as a bride adorned for her husband" (Rev. 21:2). To be her children is to have entered into the eschatological age of fulfilment through Jesus Christ.

In this connection Paul cites a prophetic text from Isaiah (54:1) which looks forward to the glory of the new Jerusalem. Because of the work of the Servant of the Lord (Isa. 53), God promises to bless His people Israel. There is a whole series of oracles in which God promises blessings richer than anything as yet experienced. This will include, though Paul does not pause to bring out the point, an ingathering of the Gentiles (55:5; 56:6 f.).

In a closing comment, Paul makes a personal application to the Galatian Christians. "Now we, like Isaac, are children of promise." Their spiritual birth had come about through the grace of God alone. Why then were the Judaizers causing them so much trouble? Paul sees another parallel in the Genesis account. Isaac was the object of Ishmael's scorn and derision (Gen. 21:9). Since we are related to Isaac, we should expect to be treated as he was. Both Jesus and Paul experienced great persecution from the unconverted Jews of their time. A religion of promise seems always to inspire hatred from a religion of works. But, nevertheless, it was Isaac, not Ishmael, who received the promise (Gen. 21:10-13). Hagar and her son were cast out. The religion of promise and the religion of works cannot coexist. God will not divide His blessing between them. All religions do not lead to God. He will exclude all who try to come to Him relying on their own achievement. Similarly, although believers are now suffering the pain of persecution as Isaac did, they are the ones who will share the privilege of inheritance as he did.

Our privilege as Christians is freedom from bondage. Yet vigilance is called for. "Stand fast therefore." We need to dig our heels deliberately into the freedom Christ has won for us so that no one will be able to drag us off into bondage again. We must take care not to slip back into the very slavery from which we have just been delivered. The "yoke of the law" was a phrase that the Jews used. Paul identifies it bluntly as the yoke of a slave. The Christian life is never a static possession. It is a dynamic experience with possibilities of growth and slipping back. We must stand fast if we expect to come into the fulness of God's blessings.

Paul's theology of the Old Testament is impressive. He sees it as a book of grace and salvation. He does not contrast it with the gospel of Jesus Christ. Rather, he finds the gospel to be the fulfilment of the central intention of the Old Testament. Salvation has always sprung from God's free grace, appropriated by simple faith.

Chapter Five

promise and fulfilment

*Now before faith came, we were confined under
the law, kept under restraint until faith should be
revealed. So that the law was our custodian until
Christ came, that we might be justified by faith.
But now that faith has come, we are no longer
under a custodian; for in Christ Jesus you are all
sons of God, through faith. For as many of you as
were baptized into Christ have put on Christ. There
is neither Jew nor Greek, there is neither slave nor
free, there is neither male nor female; for you are
all one in Christ Jesus. And if you are Christ's, then
you are Abraham's offspring, heirs according to
promise.* Galatians 3:23-29

Paul has just finished explaining the purpose and function
of the law. It is not a very happy picture. The law has
consigned all of us to sin. The purpose of this, however, is to
make us ready for grace and salvation in Christ. This is the
thought he wishes to develop now.

First, Paul likens the law to a jailor (v. 23). We were
confined by the law and kept under restraint, he writes. The
law kept us in a kind of protective custody until the time of
our release and pardon. Paul uses "faith" in a pregnant sense.
He speaks of faith coming and being revealed in Christ.
Evidently he is not thinking of faith in general. Abraham had
true and saving faith before Christ came. Paul is referring to
the faith (he uses the article). It is the faith that lays hold on
Jesus Christ.

Second, Paul talks of the law as a custodian (v. 24). This
word was used in contemporary parlance for the attendant

who escorted a child to and from school. He was not the child's teacher, though he had the power of discipline. The function of the law was to be the superintendent of human conduct, nothing more. It could rebuke and punish us for misbehavior, but do nothing to make us different. This custodial function ceased with the coming of Christ, who is able to justify and liberate sinners. The law prepared people to long for His coming.

Now that faith is operative, the custodial function of the law is finished and a new situation exists. Faith in Christ has made us God's sons and the restraints of the past are gone. Now we have grown up and have no need of a custodian. No longer are we prisoners awaiting our sentence, or children under the stern command of a tutor; we are mature sons of God with all the privileges that go with it (v. 25 f.). This is not a natural sonship based on creation. It is a sonship in Christ based on divine grace and received by faith. It is not a status we have earned by law-keeping, but a free gift to faith.

The entry into the new life in Christ was by baptism. Paul speaks of our being baptized into Christ (v. 27). In the Book of Acts baptism in Jesus' name was the act in which a convert committed himself to Christ and submitted to His authority. Baptism and faith were the inside and outside of the same thing. Inner response to the call of the gospel issued in an outward act of obedience. We cannot simply interpret baptism as a symbolic rite. The New Testament writers associate union with Christ, forgiveness of sins, the gift of the Spirit, and many other rich truths with baptism. It is not a magic rite that automatically conveys all these things, but it is an occasion when a person really encounters Jesus Christ. The reason this is so is that baptism is the external expression and crowning moment of the act of faith. It is therefore the sign of our union with the body of Christ. Baptism marks the transition from death and condemnation to a new life of peace with God and membership in the body of Christ.

Errors about baptism are legion and tragic. Some make too much of it, and others virtually ignore it. Certainly Paul, in the Galatian Epistle, is not saying baptism is the external rite which makes one a child of God. Had he believed that, his entire case against circumcision would fall to the ground. We are justified by faith in Christ, not by the religious works we perform. At the same time we must not degrade the importance of baptism. Paul teaches here that baptism is the moment of faith when a person enters into the adoption as a child of God. Most baptismal practice reduces the rite to a bare symbol, which is quite out of line with the rich apostolic teaching on the subject.

Baptized believers have "put on Christ." That is a vivid metaphor. We put on Christ as a garment. The idea here is that we enter into union with Christ so that He takes us over. Christ begins to express Himself through us. The image was used in the Old Testament. The Spirit clothed Himself with Gideon, and put on Gideon, as it were (Judg. 6:34). The personality of Christ is laid over top of our own. It helps to explain Paul's earlier words: "It is no longer I who live, but Christ who lives in me" (2:20).

Our personal union with Christ has profound social dimensions. We belong to a collective whole, the body of Christ. "You are all one person in Jesus Christ" (v. 28, NEB). All those familiar distinctions that divide the human race no longer divide people who are in Christ. Paul mentions three outstanding distinctions: the racial—"Jew or Greek"; the social—"slave or free man"; the sexual—"male or female." These distinctions make no difference in our relationship with Jesus Christ, and therefore make no profound difference at all. In Christ is to be found the most potent basis of true brotherhood. Greeks do not have to become Jews in order to be God's sons. Poor and uneducated people do not have to climb the social ladder to stand on equal ground with the elite. Women are liberated from the male domination of the past. Sexual distinctions make no difference to Christ.

Paul is calling a community in Christ, not just an aggregation of atomistic individuals. In this community of new men and women there are no privileged classes, whether clerical or racial or social. Oneness in Christ is the fundamental truth of it. And yet we are barrier ridden in our Christian congregations. We have allowed our assemblies to develop along the lines of a certain economic and racial pattern. Where is the corporate demonstration that we are all one in Christ? Believers in Christ belong to one all-inclusive person. There is no theological justification for us to make distinctions between us. The Christian community is to be the visible sign in the world of God's reconciling men to Himself and to one another. It is simply scandalous when the churches allow barriers to fellowship to arise. Sometimes prejudices persist in the church even after they have disappeared in the secular world. Truly judgment must begin with the house of God. Let us be the first, not the last, to insist that the differences which divide men do not divide us. And let us flesh it out in all manner of outward actions and expressions.

In closing Paul connects us with Abraham again. Gentiles and Jews who are in union with Jesus Christ both share in His inheritance (v. 29). We belong now to the people of God which stretch out through all the ages of world history. We are a chosen generation and a special people, as Peter says (I Peter 2:9 f.). Not only are we related to God vertically as His sons, and related to all other believers in the world horizontally; we also belong to a long line of faithful men in every age.

> *I mean that the heir, as long as he is a child, is no better than a slave, though he is the owner of all the estate; but he is under guardians and trustees until the date set by the father. So with us; when we were children, we were slaves to the elemental spirits of the universe. But when the time had fully come, God sent forth his Son, born of woman, born under the law, to redeem those who were under the law, so that we might receive adoption as sons. And because you are sons, God has sent the Spirit of his Son into our hearts, crying, "Abba! Father!" So through God you are no longer a slave but a son, and if a son then an heir.*
> *Formerly, when you did not know God, you were in bondage to beings that by nature are no gods; but now that you have come to know God or rather to be known by God, how can you turn back again to the weak and beggarly elemental spirits, whose slaves you want to be once more? You observe days, and months, and seasons, and years! I am afraid I have labored over you in vain.*
> Galatians 4:1-11

In order to prevent anyone misunderstanding his meaning, Paul rehearses the same point again, using human growth into maturity as his illustration. He wishes to compare the rights and privileges of a young child with those of a mature son. The young child, even though technically heir to a large estate, cannot receive his inheritance until he is old enough. He is no different in that respect from a slave. The heir in the years of his minority is subject to the authority of others, and his estate is managed for him by trustees. Paul is not thinking of his education and so does not introduce the "custodian" figure here. He is interested in the fact that the child has no right to administer the estate which is his by right. He has to wait until the time appointed by the father. This detail should be connected with the "fulness of time" Paul mentions later (v. 4). Christ came at the time when God decreed that mankind should come of age through faith in the gospel. Before that time Paul says we were slaves to the "elements" of the universe (v. 3).

Opinion is divided as to what this allusion means. In early Greek the term means elementary principles, even the alphabet. This seems to be the meaning it has in Hebrews 5:12. In that case Paul would be referring to the ABCs of Old Testament religion, which have now been fulfilled and transcended in Jesus Christ. Later on (v. 9) he uses the word again to denote adherence to the Jewish ritual calendar (v. 10). In the past the Jews were committed to elementary religious forms, which are now out-dated with the coming of Christ. This would be true all the more so in the case of the pagan Gentile converts. To their ears the word "elements" might have conjured up the idea of spiritual agencies to which they formerly committed themselves. Paul wants to warn the Galatians that their submission to Jewish customs would be the equivalent to returning to their former religious slavery.

It is not that the law itself is a wicked thing. God intended that the law should awaken man's sense of need and bring him to Christ and the gospel. But it had been twisted and made to serve an evil purpose. It was being used to place men into bondage and tyrannize them in a way God never intended. God uses law to bring men to Christ. Satan uses law to trap people in dark despair or delude them into thinking they can be justified by their law-keeping.

But in the fulness of time God, as an earthly father might set the limit on his son's minority, sent forth Jesus Christ. Many commentators wax eloquent on the meaning of the phrase "the fulness of time" (v. 4). They note how ready the world was to receive Christ's coming. There were Roman roads to travel by and Roman soldiers to protect the peace. The old myths and religions were losing their hold on people's minds. The Greek language and culture supplied cultural cohesion to a vast area of civilization. All of these things did much to facilitate the rapid spread of the gospel. Be that as it may, Paul's thought seems to be fixed rather on the servitude of the law and the liberty of the gospel. The time that was fulfilled was the time of God's testing of Israel under the law. During this time the hopelessness of man's condition became sufficiently obvious and the need for Christ perfectly plain. The law had served its function.

Jesus Christ is the apostle of God. He is God's missionary sent forth to rectify the sinful human condition. The verb used implies more than a bare commissioning. It means Christ was sent forth from a state in which He previously existed. He who was "in the form of God and did not consider equality with God a thing to be selfishly held on to" came forth to meet the human need (Phil. 2:6). Paul has a high doctrine of the person of Jesus Christ. He is the preexistent divine Son, "who though he was rich, for our sakes became poor" (II Cor. 8:9). The message of the gospel is the astounding proclamation of God intervening in human affairs. Although there is no answer to man's dilemmas from his own wisdom and through his own efforts, there is an answer which comes to him from beyond the human situation. "The Word became flesh and dwelt among us" (John 1:14).

Jesus Christ, sent forth from God, was also fully human— "born of a woman." This is not a reference to the virgin birth of Christ, but to His full humanity. The humanity of Christ is one of the underdeveloped doctrines of orthodox Christianity. We have been so zealous to preserve a good testimony to the deity of Christ that we have often allowed His humanity to become unreal and obscured. Yet the New Testament is eager to stress God's self-disclosure in our flesh and history. The chief Christological heresy it had to combat was docetism, the denial of His full humanity. Paul teaches that God entered fully into the conditions of human life. If we seek to modify or reduce this truth, we call into question the mode of the divine self-disclosure. God saves us, not in a display of irresistible power, but in our flesh and on a cruel cross.

Not only was Christ born as a man, He was also born under

the conditions of law. That is, He was born into the very Jewish milieu the false teachers claimed to know so much about. He had a Jewish mother, belonged to the Jewish state, was subject to Jewish law. The difference was that He succeeded where everyone else had failed. He was able to fulfil all of the law's requirements and embody its righteousness perfectly. He was born under law in order to carry out the purpose He had in coming. That purpose was twofold: to redeem us from slavery and to give us adoption status with God (v. 5). Earlier Paul mentioned our redemption through the death of Christ (3:13). Now he speaks of its results. We have been bought out of slavery and installed as sons in God's forever family. Our deliverance is from bondage unto adoption.

Then Paul refers to another divine sending. God sends the Spirit into the hearts of believers to assure them that they really possess what Christ has won for them. He comes to attest subjectively what Christ has achieved for us objectively. The Spirit's presence in our lives assures us of our sonship and enables us to pray confidently, "Abba! Father!" "Abba" was the Aramaic word which Jesus Himself used in speaking to God His Father (Mark 14:36). It is a word that suggests great intimacy. The Spirit comes to teach spiritual children how to use the language of sons instead of slaves. Every child of God receives the gift of the Spirit. There is no extra condition beyond faith to fulfil. The Spirit belongs to every believer in Jesus. Groups in our day which claim the Spirit as a personal possession and urge people to seek a special experience from God are on the wrong track. The Spirit leads people to confess Christ as Lord, and indwells all who do so (I Cor. 12:3, 13).

The trinitarian cast of Paul's teaching is noteworthy. The Son is sent forth, and then the Spirit. In this double sending we get a glimpse into the internal constitution of the Godhead. The church's doctrine of the Trinity was arrived at because the New Testament revelation required it. The Trinity was the most adequate model for expressing what Christians wanted to say about God. The Old Testament, while not without strong hints as to internal diversity within the Godhead, emphasized the unity of God over against the polytheism of surrounding cultures. The doctrine of the Trinity became visible only after events occurred which required a trinitarian God as their cause. The revelation in word, such as we find here, had to await the revelation in fact, namely the incarnation and Pentecost.

In the ministry of Jesus Christ and in the experience of the early church, trinitarian divine reality was encountered. God the Father, Jesus the Lord, and the Holy Spirit all designate a single divine reality, and yet operate in such a way as to imply a personal distinction between them. New Testament theism is trinitarian theism. This doctrine is an inference we have to draw as to the nature of God from what we know God to be in His own self-disclosure. If we give full cognitive authority to the apostle here, we have to be trinitarian in our theology. Our stewardship of the Word of God carries us in that direction. Of course we do not pretend to know more about this profound mystery than we really do. We want to say no more about it than God Himself has shown us in Scripture. Neither do we want to say less.

God has secured our sonship by His Son, and assures us of it by His Spirit. Christ has won this status for us, and the Spirit comes into our hearts to give us the experience of it. "So *through God you are no longer a slave but a son, and if a son then* an heir" (v. 7). We are God's sons and heirs, but this relationship is not accomplished through any effort on our part or any personal worth. It is God's action in sending Son and Spirit that is responsible for our salvation.

Then Paul makes a personal appeal to the Galatians not to lapse back into bondage. If we are God's sons, he pleads, let us live like the sons we are. Having come to know God through Christ, how can we even contemplate returning to legalistic bondage again? In their pre-Christian state the Galatians were slaves to nongods (v. 8). Because God created heaven and earth, the other so-called gods identified with various created elements could not be gods in the true sense of the word. The great sin of lost man is his worship of the creature rather than the creator (Rom. 1:25). But now that the Galatians have come to know the living God, everything has changed (v. 9).

The verb "to know" in the Bible has a far deeper meaning than intellectual knowledge alone. It is used of the intimate way a husband knows his wife. Similarly, we know God in a way that goes far beyond knowing *about* God. Then Paul checks his language. He adds the phrase "or rather to be known by God." Coming to know God is one way to speak of conversion. Becoming the objects of God's knowledge is another. The first expression might give the impression that the Galatian converts had sought God out and found Him by their own unaided efforts. In actual fact, God is actively drawing men to Christ, so it is He who has made Himself known by God." Coming to know God is one way to speak divine initiative in salvation. In the light of this, Paul wants to know, how can the Galatians even consider turning back to pseudogods?

Paul characterizes pagan religions as "weak and beggarly elements" (v. 9). His emphasis falls on the powerlessness and poverty of those systems to deliver men from bondage and bring them to the true God. Evidently he did not think of these religions as more or less helpful in introducing men to salvation. The Galatians, to be sure, did not believe accepting the Jewish law was the equivalent of returning to pagan religion. But Paul is convinced that it is. He wants them to have no doubt as to what the dire consequences of this action would be. He wishes to shock them into a realization of what, howbeit unknowingly, they were at that moment contemplating. "You observe days and months and seasons and years." These "days" could refer to the liturgical calendar of orthodox Judaism. They could equally refer to pagan festivals in the religions of Asia Minor. Even today, with the popularity of horoscopes, the concept of the "lucky day" is not unknown. Paul was appalled to think that the Galatian Christians might turn from Christ to empty and superstitious formalism. However appealing the false teachers may have made it sound, Paul sees it simply as a return to slavery.

Paul underlines the full seriousness of the situation in this closing comment: "I am afraid I have labored over you in vain" (v. 11; cf. 3:4). He wonders to himself whether all the toil he underwent preaching to them and all the spiritual experiences they had known were wasted. Did all this effort result in nothing? Paul did not regard the possibility of apostasy as only a theoretical and not a real danger. The security of the Galatian believers was not unconditional. Certain beliefs and practices, if adopted with wide open eyes, would certainly land the Galatians beyond the pale of salvation. Scripture gives us the basis of an assurance of the strongest possible kind. But it also repeatedly warns us against pre-

sumption; that is, against an assurance divorced from discipleship. Only believers who persevere have any right to assurance. Christ's parable of the sower makes Paul's point clearly.
It speaks of some who hear the Word, receive it with joy, and
believe for a while, but in a time of temptation fall away
(Luke 8:13). The very purpose of Galatians is to warn believers of the dread possibility of final apostasy. Hebrews
deals with the same problem in another setting. There is in
our churches far too much cheap assurance. We do not hear
the strong warnings which the New Testament addresses to
believers. People do not want to question the doctrine of
"eternal security." How else could they enjoy assurance
while doing a shoddy job of discipleship? Countless profess-
ing Christians today need to hear about their precarious
standing and enter into lives of serious discipleship. "Not
every one who says to me, 'Lord, Lord,' shall enter the
kingdom of heaven, but he who does the will of my Father
who is in heaven" (Matt. 7:21). If we call Christ Master and
do not treat Him as such, we will not be finally saved.

Let us notice the flow of Paul's argument here. Once we
were slaves (vv. 1-3); now we are God's sons (vv. 4-7); let us
remember who we are and act like sons (vv. 8-11)! Quite
frequently Paul makes an appeal to the mind in the interests
of Christian holiness (Rom. 6:3; I Cor. 6:16). If we would
but remember who we are, perhaps we would act according-
ly. "As a man thinks in his heart, so is he." Holy thinking
leads to holy living. Let us remember that we are sons, and
judge our own behavior in that light.

Chapter Six

a pastor's dilemma

*Brethren, I beseech you, become as I am, for I also
have become as you are. You did me no wrong;
you know it was because of a bodily ailment that I
preached the gospel to you at first; and though my
condition was a trial to you, you did not scorn or
despise me, but received me as an angel of God, as
Christ Jesus. What has become of the satisfaction
you felt? For I bear you witness that, if possible,
you would have plucked out your eyes and given
them to me. Have I then become your enemy by
telling you the truth? They make much of you, but
for no good purpose; they want to shut you out,
that you may make much of them. For a good
purpose it is always good to be made much of, and
not only when I am present with you. My little
children, with whom I am again in travail until
Christ be formed in you! I could wish to be present
with you now and to change my tone, for I am
perplexed about you.* Galatians 4:12-20

Up until now we have seen chiefly the stern side of Paul's
character. We have seen the strength of his convictions and
his willingness to uphold gospel truth against any and all
attempts to pervert it. He seems to prefer truth to peace, as
on the occasion when he rebuked Peter publicly. The argument of the epistle has been somewhat impersonal up to this
point, as Paul the theologian grapples with principles and
concepts. But here the letter takes a personal direction. He
calls the Galatians his brothers and his little children, the

strongest terms of affection he has yet allowed himself to use. In this passage we catch a glimpse of another, gentler side to Paul's personality. Now we meet Paul the man and loving pastor. We learn too some important principles which ought to govern the relations between pastor and people.

As he appealed to the Galatians not to return to bondage, Paul was reminded of his missionary labors among them and his warmth of love toward them personally. "Brethren, I beseech you"—he writes in a mood of intense longing. "Become as I am, for I also have become as you are" (v. 12). Paul is asking the Galatians to put themselves in his shoes, and to show him the kind of consideration he had shown them. We do not know the exact details of this, but the reference is probably to Paul's missionary style. He sought to be all things to all men, to identify wherever possible with those he wished to reach (I Cor. 9:19-23). When with the Galatians Paul had not stood on his dignity and kept his distance, refusing to mingle with the people. No, he identified with them in their difficulties and needs. Now he asks them to show him the same kind of loving empathy in this situation. If they would only look at this problem from his point of view, they would easily understand his feelings in the matter and not take the attitude they have.

Paul reviews their earlier attitude toward him. He had nothing at all to complain about. "You did me no wrong" (v. 12). This was especially noteworthy because of a personal incident which Paul alludes to. Evidently, at the time of his work among the Galatians, Paul was suffering from some kind of malady. He does not say what it was. We can only guess as to its nature, so there is no point speculating what it might have been. We know the condition was a "trial" to the Galatians and may have had something to do with his eyesight (v. 15). Whatever the weakness was, the Galatians did not despise Paul for it, but received him as God's angel (v. 14). They couldn't have received Christ any better!

Paul's point is that the Galatians received him at the first just as they should—as the messenger of Jesus Christ bearing the word of God. He says that in order to contrast it with their present attitude toward him. At one time they accepted him as God's emissary and believed the word he brought. Now they seem to have doubts. Their earlier attitude was the right one. They did not yield to the temptation to judge the message and the messenger by outward appearances. They received God's word gladly. Now it seems as if they pay their respects to the Judaizers.

But all that is past. "What became of the satisfaction you felt?" (v. 15). Once upon a time the Galatians had considered themselves blessed to have Paul ministering in their midst. They would have gone to any lengths to show their appreciation to him. The eye is a symbol of the body's most precious possession, and they were willing to pluck out their eyes and give them to him. Some see this as proof Paul suffered from some eye disease. Constant study in poor light made for a high incidence of eye trouble in the first century Mediterranean world. The Galatians were prepared to give Paul their own eyes to help him do his work. Of course we do not know that he suffered from eye problems. There is no need to see more in the language than the extravagant devotion of convert to teacher. But now the pleasure they once felt in his ministry has vanished. Their attitude to him had become hostile. Why was that?

The change came about because he told them some unpalatable truth. "Have I then become your enemy by telling you the truth?" (v. 16). Speaking the truth in love is a Christian virtue but is not always welcomed. When Paul told the Galatians some painful truths, they completely changed their attitude toward him. Like so many of us, their enthusiasm for a Bible teacher dried up as soon as he got onto some unwelcome subjects which convicted them. They wished to be selective in their obedience to Christian truths, accepting those they liked and ignoring the rest. They needed to learn a lesson. The authority of God's Word does not disappear when an unpleasant teaching is encountered. God's Word has authority in whatever it teaches, whether we happen to like it or not.

In the following verses Paul compares the attitude of the false teachers toward the Galatians with his own. They fussed over them and flattered them. Three times Paul uses a verb that is difficult to translate. It means "to have a deep concern over someone" of a good or a bad kind. The Judaizers made much of the Galatians, but they had an evil purpose in mind. They were trying to shut the Galatians out of the sphere of God's grace (v. 17). In their case their concern was more like "envy." They were jealous of the freedom the Galatians enjoyed and wished to bring an end to it.

The verb "to shut out" (v. 17) is related to a verb used earlier (3:22). The law herded men together so that they might find salvation. The Judaizers, however, are locking men out lest they find it. There could not be a greater contrast than between the purpose of the law and the purposes of the false teachers. They wish to wean the Galatians away from Paul and the gospel, and make them slaves to the law and disciples of themselves. There is nothing wrong in being treated royally if it is in the interests of a good purpose, Paul says (v. 18). In fact, when he was with them he gave them careful attention and lavished his time on them. He only could wish they felt the same way toward him now in his absence as they did when he was present. He confesses not to know what to think. "I am perplexed about you" (v. 20).

Paul's attitude to the Galatians was very different from that of the false teachers. He had no desire to take advantage of them. He speaks of himself as a mother in the pangs of childbirth, so great is his concern for their welfare (v. 19). He was in travail until Christ should be "formed in" them. He calls them his little children. He had no desire, as the Judaizers did, to have control over them or use them for his own personal prestige. They were his converts, the fruit of his labor in Christ. He was their spiritual father through the gospel (cf. I Cor. 4:15). He was not a father in the sense that the Galatians ought to be spiritually dependent on him (cf. Matt. 23:8). Our converts ought to depend on Christ, not on us. These parental images express the compassion and concern Paul felt toward them. Elsewhere Paul can speak of himself as a nurse (I Thess. 2:8).

Paul likens his concern in this instance to the pangs of childbirth. The metaphor is apt. He is a Christian pastor watching anxiously for signs of spiritual growth in his people. This was "the daily pressure upon me of my anxiety for all the churches" (II Cor. 11:28). He wants to see Christ, like an embryo, be formed in the believers. If the metaphor is a little mixed, the point is clear. He is not satisfied that Christ should simply dwell in them. He wants to see Christ formed in them. The New English Bible turns the metaphor around: "until you take the shape of Christ." This translation is a bit free with Paul's language, but quite true to his theology. Paul's aim was not simply to get people converted, but to see them grow into a Christ-like character.

If we pay attention to this little-known passage of Galatians, we will pick up some valuable hints as to the proper relation between pastor and people. First, as to the pastor, Calvin wrote, "If ministers wish to do any good, let them labour to form Christ, not to form themselves, in their hearers." Paul wanted Jesus Christ to control the lives of the Galatians. He was worried about their spiritual growth, not his own advancement or reputation. He was willing to undergo much pain and agony that God's people might mature in their spiritual walk.

These ought to be the aims of modern pastors as well. Let them be concerned about the welfare of their people and their spiritual progress, and now their own careers. Let them seek how to serve them, not to exploit them. Paul was perplexed how he could do this. He had to weigh his concern for the truth over against his love and concern for the Galatians themselves. Being a pastor is not the kind of job a person should seek out for his own comfort and enjoyment. Its satisfactions are gained through much effort and pain.

There are lessons here for congregations also. The people should not judge their leader by outward appearance. He may be intelligent or average, eloquent or dull, handsome or ugly. These are not the important things. They should neither flatter him because he is gifted nor despise him because he is not. They should not assess his worth according to their favorite teachings. He is a minister of the Word of God. That is his dignity and his responsibility. Our attitude toward him should be determined only by his fidelity to the letter and spirit of the revealed message. If he is faithful to the gospel, his ministry should be humbly and gratefully received, not because of his office but because his message is the message of Jesus Christ.

Our modern congregations are as fickle in these matters as the Galatians were. How often a preacher is criticized for how long he preaches, or how his family dresses, or what he feels led to say. The only legitimate cause for criticism would be if he were not faithful in word or deed to the apostolic gospel. If he is true to his commission as a minister of God's Word, he deserves our love and respect. How often it is that a congregation, in calling a pastor, will look for a dozen other qualities in a man before they inquire after his doctrinal convictions—if they ever do. Most congregations today need to be more alert, more humble, and more hungry in listening to the exposition of God's Word.

Of course it is true that a pastor today is not an apostle of Jesus Christ. He does not have that kind of authority or authorization. He should not act, and the people should not treat him, as if he were. Yet he is called to teach the people the apostolic message. And if he is true to this calling, the people's attitude to him ought to reflect their attitude to Christ and His apostles.

Chapter Seven

only two religions

Now I, Paul, say to you that if you receive circumcision, Christ will be of no advantage to you. I testify again to every man who receives circumcision that he is bound to keep the whole law. You are severed from Christ, you who would be justified by the law; you have fallen away from grace. For through the Spirit, by faith, we wait for the hope of righteousness. For in Christ Jesus neither circumcision nor uncircumcision is of any avail, but faith working through love. You were running well; who hindered you from obeying the truth? This persuasion is not from him who called you. A little leaven leavens the whole lump. I have confidence in the Lord that you will take no other view than mine; and he who is troubling you will bear his judgment, whoever he is. But if I, brethren, still preach circumcision, why am I still persecuted? In that case the stumbling block of the cross has been removed. I wish those who unsettle you would mutilate themselves! Galatians 5:2-12

In this polemical section the issues are drawn exceedingly clear. There are only two religions in the world: the religion of human achievement, represented here by circumcision, and the religion of divine grace. There is no other alternative; we must receive one or the other. Will we magnify our own accomplishments, or humbly bow beneath the cross of Jesus?

But it is far more than simply an attack on the Judaizers for compelling the Galatians to accept circumcision. It introduces to the reader a new line of argument. The gospel is able to bring about a complete inner change in believers which all the restraints of the law failed to produce. Any outward observance is impotent to effect the change which can come about through the working of the Holy Spirit.

Paul begins his remarks in an unusually solemn way: "I, Paul" (v. 2) and "I testify again" (v. 3). He would tell the Galatians something of the greatest weight. The rite of circumcision is what he had in mind. Up until now Paul has been concentrating on central principles, and has not referred explicitly to circumcision. Evidently this was the practical question where the principles had to be tested.

To us in our situation the question of circumcision seems nothing to get upset about. For us, it is merely a surgical operation for purposes of hygiene. But for Paul and the Galatians, circumcision was a ceremonial rite with profound theological implications. It stood for a religious philosophy in which human works were determinative for salvation. The circumcision-party put it this way: "Unless you are circumcised and keep the law, you cannot be saved" (Acts 15:2). The tense of the verb Paul uses gives this sense: "If you should now accept circumcision." The Galatians were contemplating this step, but had not yet taken it. The motive, were they to do so, would be the belief that the rite was necessary to salvation. His advice to them is identical to that given to the Corinthian Christians: "Was anyone at the time of his call uncircumcised? Let him not seek circumcision" (I Cor. 7:18). For a Gentile to seek circumcision would mean he regarded faith in Christ as insufficient for receiving salvation. The epistle has an urgent tone because Paul believes it is still possible to stop the Galatians from taking this fateful step.

If the Galatians were to give in to this temptation, they would nullify everything Christ did for them. We do not have to merit the merit of Christ; indeed we cannot do so. Paul uses a strong expression: "Christ will do you no good." Paul wants to shock them into realizing the seriousness of the move they are considering. He employs a pun to drive the point home. The verb in the phrase "Christ will not *benefit* you" (v. 2) and the noun in the phrase "he is *debtor* to keep the whole law" (v. 3) are from the same root. We might bring it out in English this way: "So far from Christ helping you, you yourself will be helpless in the law's clutches." Accepting the belief that some human work is necessary for justification is an act of apostasy from Christ. It would judge His work inadequate and incomplete. It is incompatible with saving faith.

Having shown the Galatians what they would lose by accepting circumcision—namely, the benefits of Christ's redemption—Paul now shows them what they would gain. They would acquire the obligation to keep the entire law, an unenviable burden to have to bear. His reasoning goes something like this: accepting circumcision would mean trusting Christ was not enough; there is something we have to do to be saved. So they would enter in upon another way of justification, by human efforts and law-keeping. But a person cannot be justified in two ways at once, by grace and by works. A person who accepted circumcision, hoping to save himself thereby, would have left the sphere in which grace is operative and become severed from Christ. It is impossible at one moment to accept Christ, admitting one cannot save himself, and at the next receive circumcision, implying one can and must. If one tries to add anything to Christ, he loses Christ and drops out of the sphere where grace operates.

It was not just circumcision the Judaizers were demanding. They wanted the Galatians to observe the whole gamut of Jewish festivals (4:10). The encounter with Peter makes it highly likely Jewish food laws were involved too (2:12). To the Judaizers, circumcision was the first step of obedience to a law which from then on would rule a person's life in every detail. Through complete obedience to its every precept, the legalist would hope to win merit in God's eyes. That kind of theology breaks the bond of faith in God's unmerited grace. The Galatians were in danger of losing Christ Himself. Their security was conditioned on their abiding in Christ. But if they turn away from Him, they lose their right to salvation. "If a man does not abide in me, he is cast forth as a branch and withers" (John 15:6).

Paul begins his next sentence (v. 5) with the pronoun "we" in a very prominent position. Up to this point he had been speaking of "you"—the Galatians contemplating accepting the law. Now he speaks of "we"—evangelical believers who wish to stand fast in the grace of God and the liberty of Christ; "through the Spirit, by faith, we wait for the hope of righteousness." The Spirit and faith—these are the two features of the gospel that distinguish it so clearly from works-religion. Circumcision was a work of flesh, not Spirit. It is something man does for himself.

The dynamic of Christian existence is the Spirit, not the flesh. Salvation is the work of God from beginning to end. The Spirit convinces us that we cannot commend ourselves to God by our own activities, and enables us to hear the gospel witness as the Word of God that it is. Faith points us again to what we do: nothing. Elsewhere Paul explains: "It depends on faith, in order that the promise may rest on grace" (Rom. 4:16). In making salvation conditional on a faith response, God ensures that the grace principle is preserved. In Spirit and faith we see the nice balance which Scripture maintains between God's action and man's response.

Paul says we are eagerly waiting for the hope of righteousness. The Christian religion is future oriented. Although salvation has been made available in the gospel, its future consummation remains unfulfilled. We have a theology of hope. "According to his promise we wait for new heavens and a new earth in which righteousness dwells" (II Peter 3:13). We have been justified by faith already (Rom. 5:1), but that declaration of right standing with God awaits public vindication at the judgment seat of Christ. We know what the future holds, but we do not on that account cease to wait eagerly for it. Believers live in joyful confidence of eschatological glory.

Think of what that means for our message to the world. All men live in hope. They cannot rest satisfied with the past or the present. Their hope for the future frequently transcends any of the immediate causes for hope. Modern man strives for a basis which will justify his own irrepressible hope. To this we respond that there is a ground for hope. Human life has a meaning and man has a destiny. That hope is grounded in God's unshakable love. "I am sure that neither death, nor life, nor angels, nor principalities, nor things present, nor things to come, nor powers, nor height, nor depth, nor anything else in all creation, will be able to separate us from the love of God in Christ Jesus our Lord" (Rom. 8:38 f.).

In the next verse Paul's true greatness shines through. "In Christ Jesus neither circumcision nor uncircumcision is of any avail, but faith working through love" (v. 6). Even in the midst of a fierce controversy he is not one-sided. Uncircumcision was as valueless as circumcision. He will not permit boasting on either side. We may compare the way he deals with a similar problem at Corinth: "Food will not commend us to God. We are no worse off if we do not eat, and no better off if we do" (I Cor. 8:8).

That kind of balanced perspective is what we need in the church today. If only we could keep our eyes fixed on the things that really matter. These outward observances are all so inconsequential compared with "faith working through love." Faith in Christ, a living relationship with Him, must issue forth in acts of love which fulfil the law. Here Paul touches on a theme that will occupy him later in this chapter. A faith response to the gospel will lead to the very righteousness which the law by itself vainly seeks to produce. Paul and James are in perfect agreement. Justifying faith is not a barren intellectual understanding. It is a confidence in God which is fruitful in concrete acts of righteousness.

Paul has begun by comparing two kinds of believers. Now he contrasts himself with the false teachers. "You were running well; who hindered you from obeying the truth?" (v. 7). Paul likes to think of Christian growth in terms of athletics. He sees the Christian life as a strenuous contest to gain a prize (cf. I Cor. 9:24-27). The Galatians had been making progress in the Christian race, until someone put an obstruction in their path. The effect was to hinder them following the plain truth of the gospel. Who was it that got them to retire from the race? Certainly not God! "This persuasion is not from him who called you" (v. 8). God called them by His grace and received them by faith. He would never lead them to forsake the gospel. The idea did not originate with Him.

Once again Paul plays on his words. The verb "obeying" (v. 7) is related to the noun "persuasion" (v. 8). To bring out the thought, we might render it in this way: "Who hindered you from being *persuaded* of the truth? This *persuasion* is not from him who called you. . . . I am *persuaded* in the Lord" (vv. 7, 8, 10). This use of a single Greek root gives the passage a coherence that is difficult to duplicate in English.

In this connection Paul cites a proverb. "A little leaven leavens the whole lump" (v. 9). The proverb draws our attention to the fact that a little false doctrine can easily spread and contaminate the whole church. The proverb, cited also in I Corinthians 5:6, measures the influence of apparently insignificant factors in the moral and spiritual realm. Up till now the Judaizers may have had little success persuading the Galatians. But Paul sees a great potential danger in the activities of the Judaizers. In time they could so affect the whole church that it would be too late to do anything about it. This is not heresy-hunting. Paul is just clear-sighted enough to see the disastrous consequences which will inevitably flow from this danger if it goes unchecked. The influence of the error was spreading, and Paul was determined to resist it.

Though the danger of apostasy is real, Paul feels personally convinced the error is not going to triumph. "I have confidence in the Lord that you will take no other view than mine" (v. 10). Paul adds the phrase "in the Lord" because the confidence he has was one which the Lord gave him. He wants the Galatians to know that, though he has had to speak sternly to them in this letter, he has not given up on them and is convinced they will see the light. He is convinced they will not make a mistake and swallow the Judaizers' line. He is also certain that the persons harassing them will receive God's judgment, whoever they are, however exalted their rank. The verb "to bear" which Paul uses is interesting. Peter used it at the Council of Jerusalem in reference to bearing the yoke of the law (Acts 15:10). The Judaizers who are so keen to have the Galatians *bear* the legal yoke will have to *bear* the much heavier burden of God's judgment.

In the next verse Paul makes a remark which suggests someone actually had claimed that he, Paul, advocated circumcision! "But if I, brethren, still preach circumcision, why am I still persecuted?" (v. 11). Who could it be? It could be that someone had heard of his subjecting Timothy to circumcision on one occasion (Acts 16:3). But nothing could support the charge he "heralded abroad" circumcision! At any rate Paul refutes it. If that were so, why would he still be suffering persecution from the Judaizers everywhere he went? That persecution results from his preaching of the cross. The "scandal of the cross" is a central concept in Paul's theology. Calling the cross a "scandal" points to the fact that it arouses opposition and creates an offense. "We preach Christ crucified, a stumbling block to Jews and folly to Gentiles" (I Cor. 1:23).

Why is this so? It is because the cross leaves no room at all for pride in human achievement. Salvation is all of grace through faith, and not at all from human merit. Therefore, to preach Christ is to invite persecution because it is offensive to be told that God must save us, that we cannot save ourselves. The message of the cross is despised because it brings proud man low and demands that he accept a free gift he could in no way deserve. People do not like to be told that they are helpless sinners who deserve only judgment and can do nothing to save themselves. It is much less offensive to preach circumcision. That opens the door to human achievement again and tells man he can do something on his behalf to win God's favor. God's way of salvation leaves no room for merit acquired by such outward observances as circumcision. The natural man always finds "staggering" God's way of salvation. It transcends his natural reasoning and understanding. To be a Christian is to glory precisely in the scandal of the cross (6:14).

Paul's final rejoinder to the Judaizers shocks many modern students of Paul. He tells them, in effect, that if they are so enthusiastic about circumcision, why don't they go all the way and castrate themselves, just like the pagan priests of Asia Minor do in honor of their gods. Let them turn the knives on themselves. The language is strong, but the point is well made. For a Gentile, circumcision could have little more significance than the other ritual cuttings and markings practiced in the ancient world.

Circumcision was a sign of God's covenant with Israel. But it is not His sign of covenant with us. It has no more relevance to Gentile Christians than any other strange custom they might come across. Paul's expression conveys his deep disgust at what the Judaizers were trying to do. His words offend our sensitive ears. But is it because we care for God and the gospel more than he did? Paul yearns for the removal of false teachers from the scene so that God's truth can be preserved and His church grow. There is no getting around the fact that the Epistle to the Galatians is deeply polemical. In our age of easy tolerance, people believe so few things deeply that they cannot get excited about any deviation from the gospel. Truth matters profoundly for Paul. He sees serious error threatening the church, and is determined to resist it. We all stand in his debt.

Chapter Eight

the way of holiness

> *For you were called to freedom, brethren; only do
> not use your freedom as an opportunity for the
> flesh, but through love be servants of one another.
> For the whole law is fulfilled in one word, "You
> shall love your neighbor as yourself." But if you
> bite and devour one another take heed that you
> are not consumed by one another.*
> *But I say, walk by the Spirit, and do not gratify
> the desires of the flesh. For the desires of the flesh
> are against the Spirit, and the desires of the Spirit
> are against the flesh; for these are opposed to each
> other, to prevent you from doing what you would.
> But if you are led by the Spirit you are not under
> the law.* Galatians 5:13-18

Paul's preoccupation thus far in Galatians has been to
emphasize the gratuitous character of God's salvation
through Christ. Now he launches into a major section to
show how faith in Christ leads to a fulfilment of God's righteousness in human life. No doubt the Judaizers charged Paul
with antinomianism, as if he told believers they could live in
any way they wished. To answer that charge, and to complete his discussion of Christian existence, Paul takes up the
question of Christian holiness. He goes into several questions:
how freedom is to be used (vv. 13-18); the contrast between
the old life-style and the Spirit filled life (vv. 19-23); the
transformed interpersonal relations required (5:24—6:5); the
principle of sowing and reaping written into the whole of life
(6:6-10).

Christ has indeed called us unto liberty (5:1), but Christian liberty is not license to do anything one wants to. Paul has to tell his readers the true nature and proper uses of freedom. "Freedom" is one of those words on everyone's lips today which has a great multiplicity of meanings. Evidently this was so in Paul's day. The Galatians had not yet grasped the true nature of Christian freedom. Some of them thought it was synonymous with moral anarchy. They saw in it a golden opportunity to indulge their sinful appetites. Paul warns them against that. "Do not use your freedom as an opportunity for the flesh" (v. 13). His language pictures freedom being used as a "base of operations" for the lower nature. People were using their liberty as a pretext for fallen human nature ("flesh") to express itself. They did not see the difference between freedom *from* sin and freedom *to* sin!

In actual fact, Christian freedom entails definite moral obligations. Though we are not slaves to the law or to sin, we are called to serve God and one another: "through love be servants of one another." The Christian is like the freed slave who refuses to leave the household of the master he loves, but chooses to serve him forever (Exod. 21:1-6). The service is voluntary, the compulsion one of love.

Evidently the Galatians had not grasped the principle of loving service. Paul refers to savage infighting which went on in their congregation (v. 15). He speaks of them biting and devouring each other. Both verbs are used of the habits of wild animals. Apparently the behavior of the Galatians at times resembled the conduct more fitting to untamed beasts than to brothers in Christ. Paul may be thinking of the savage scavenger dogs which fed on the garbage of cities in his day. That kind of behavior promotes self-destruction. We have been called to love and serve people, not to use and abuse them as objects for our own advantage.

Paul justifies this principle of love for the neighbor from the Old Testament law (Lev. 19:18; cf. Luke 10:27). Love is both a summary of the law and a carrying out of its deepest intentions (cf. Rom. 13:8-10). Love of the neighbor is not just another commandment, it is the sum total of the moral attitude toward others. Moreover, it is the mode in which love for God is fleshed out. The Levite, in the Good Samaritan parable, who did not care for the needy neighbor did not truly love God either. "He who does not love his brother whom he has seen, cannot love God whom he has not seen"

(I John 4:20). We are to love God by and through loving the neighbor. There is no reason to think the Judaizers would have disagreed with this idea. The law requires love for the neighbor.

There is a profound difference between Paul's concept of law being fulfilled by love and the new morality's concept of law being negated by it. The new morality sees in love the basis for breaking God's laws. Paul sees in love the way to fulfil them. In the new morality love is divorced from revealed standards of conduct. It becomes an autonomous principle to invoke in any situation. Taken that way, the content of love becomes a problem. Imagine inviting a builder to construct the kind of house "the site required"! We would need to be more specific. The site could accommodate several different kinds of houses. What the new morality actually does is to smuggle secular norms of action into ethical situations without admitting it. It does not actually operate by "love alone." It infuses love with the content called for by the contemporary cultural consensus.

How does Paul's position differ from this? For him, love is the fulfilment of the law, but the law as adapted and mediated through Jesus Christ. The temporary aspects of the law have been set aside. Its demands have to be read in the light of messianic revelation. Paul's view differs both from that of the new morality and that of the Judaizers. Against the new morality, Paul contends the law does have a didactic function for the believer. It can define the moral obligation for him. There are divinely revealed standards of conduct. But against the Judaizers, Paul insists that the law is not now and never was intended to be the instrument of salvation. Furthermore, the Mosaic legislation was given for the time prior to the coming of Christ and is not now in effect as such. Righteousness is now mediated through Jesus Christ. Messianic revelation supersedes everything else. But it does not do so out of all continuity with the past. It abstracts out of the law the principles of inner righteousness and subsumes them under the "law of Christ."

How are the Galatians to check their tendency to devour each other? How can they control their runaway self-centeredness and learn to give themselves freely in loving service to others? The answer is the Spirit controlled life (v. 16). If they would walk in the Spirit, they would not fulfill the answer the call of the lower nature. Paul is not telling them to do something they have not done before. He is urging them to keep on walking in the Spirit day by day. This is the secret of Christian holiness.

Paul describes the Christian life as a conflict of opposing forces. What the Spirit yearns for in our lives is antithetical to what the lower nature desires (v. 17). A civil war rages within the believer. Peter wrote about it: "Beloved, I beseech you as aliens and exiles to abstain from the passions of the flesh that wage war against your soul" (I Peter 2:11). The Spirit and the flesh are implacable foes. Paul's teaching makes it impossible to accept "quietism," the theory that sanctification does not require effort or struggle on our part. All we have to do is surrender to God and let Him have the victory over sin. While it is true that God sanctifies us, it is not true that a person being renewed by the Spirit exists in a state of passive surrender. God has done everything to make our sanctification possible, but we must make our calling and election sure by putting to death the old life and walking in the Spirit.

Paul does not teach here what is called the doctrine of the "two natures" in the believer—the idea that we are spectators to a tug-of-war between the old and the new natures within us. What he presents is the decision that faces all of us, whether to sow to the flesh or to the Spirit. We are faced with two directions in which to walk. The spiritual conflict we experience is our own personal striving against the Spirit of God. Paul urges us to walk consistently after the Spirit and in the Spirit. Whichever we do, we do in the whole person. The consequences of the choice are eternal (6:8).

Paul understands the Christian life to be a life of being led along by the Spirit (v. 18). Only He can give the strength to subdue our sinful passions and cause the fruit of righteousness to grow in our lives. The Spirit is the divine guide to whom we are to submit ourselves. This chapter is crammed with references to His working. We are under Him, not under law.

> *Now the works of the flesh are plain: immorality, impurity, licentiousness, idolatry, sorcery, enmity, strife, jealousy, anger, selfishness, dissension, party spirit, envy, drunkenness, carousing, and the like. I*

warn you, as I warned you before, that those who do such things shall not inherit the kingdom of God. But the fruit of the Spirit is love, joy, peace, patience, kindness, goodness, faithfulness, gentleness, self-control; against such there is no law.
Galatians 5:19-23

In this passage Paul contrasts the kinds of behavior that are characterized by the absence and presence of the Spirit in turn. First he supplies a catalogue of vices which were common in his day and by no means foreign to our own. If he seems a little severe in his judgment, we should remember that pagan moralists were, if anything, more severe in their criticism. What fallen human nature produces is "plain" for all to see, qualities which are astonishingly up to date.

The list seems to divide into four general areas. First there is the category of sexual vices: "immorality, impurity, licentiousness" (v. 19). Sexual life, like everything else, has become disordered by the fall of man into sin. These vices were as notorious and evident in Paul's day as they are in our own. In his day sexual irregularities were often connected with religious rites, compounding sensuality with blasphemy. Paul is not antisexual in his teaching. Sex is the good gift of God, its proper place being in the permanent marriage relationship. Perverted and promiscuous sexual activity, however, is displeasing to God and harmful to human dignity and relationships.

Second, there is the category of religious sins: "idolatry, sorcery" (v. 20). The works of the flesh operate in many realms beyond the sexual. False religion is every bit as much a work of the flesh as adultery. Indeed, the Bible frequently connects idolatry with immorality. Men are idolatrous when they put something in God's place and worship it as ultimate. It may not involve polytheism at all. Race, nationality, money, even work can all take God's place in our lives. Sorcery had special relevance for the Galatians living in Asia Minor (cf. Acts 19:19). It refers to the use of magic charms and superstitious rites designed to tap the powers of the spirit world. The term literally means "the use of drugs." Magic and early forms of medicine were closely related. Drugs are being used in our day to simulate religious experiences, a secular attempt to counterfeit the gifts of the Spirit of God.

Third, there are the sins of society: "enmity, strife, jealousy, anger, selfishness, dissension, party spirit, envy" (20 f.). These vices had particular relevance to the Galatian situation. They had great trouble getting along together (v. 15). Sin creates chaos in interpersonal relationships. Sin leads people to radical self-centeredness, which in turn results in conflict and bitterness. A casual reflection on the events in daily life will reveal the tragic presence of all of these vices in what people do and say. It is doubly sad when these very same divisive attitudes crop up even in our Christian communities.

Finally, there are sins in the realm of drink: "drunkenness, carousing" (v. 21). Drunken orgies frequently took place at the festivals of the pagan gods. Some drunkenness even crept into the Corinthian love-feast (I Cor. 11:21). This kind of self-indulgence is yet another proof of the carnal life.

Paul made no effort to make his list complete. He simply selected a number of sinful activities to illustrate his point. At the end of the list Paul repeats a warning he must have given during his preaching among the Galatians. Doing things such as these can bar a person from entering the kingdom of God. Such attitudes and actions give clear proof that a person is not abiding in Christ and walking in His Spirit. Their presence attests a lack of spiritual reality. We cannot get ourselves off the hook by saying "true" Christians would not engage in this sort of thing. Paul's point is much stronger. If professed believers—all of whom consider themselves "true" Christians—engage in this kind of living, they will not in the end inherit eschatological blessing.

In sharp contrast Paul now presents a list of spiritual virtues. The use of the metaphor of "fruit" is suggestive, as it places emphasis on spontaneous growth from within. It is also a singular, not a plural, noun. The work of the Spirit produces a cluster of fine fruit, a moral diamond with nine sides. If we wish to know what are the normative signs of the fulness of the Spirit in a person's life, here they are. The gifts for service in the body of Christ are of infinite variety and given to individuals according to God's will (I Cor. 12:7, 11, 29). They are not the proof of true spirituality. The Corinthians gloried in their gifts and were carnal Christians (I Cor. 3:1). The normative sign of the Spirit's fulness in a believer is not some impressive, even flashy, gift. It is the ethical and spiritual renewal which gradually comes to characterize the person who is led by the Spirit.

It is unlikely that Paul intended any strict divisions in this list. The first three—"love, joy, peace"—read like an adapted Jewish greeting. Our love for God is fundamental. From it stems our joy, which is independent of temporal circumstances, and our peace, with God and in ourselves. What a lovely contrast with the chaotic conditions that exist in the life of the person walking according to the flesh. The second three—"patience, kindness, goodness"—should characterize our attitude to other people. We are to learn to put up with people even when they are trying our patience. This was something Paul needed a great deal of in dealing with the Galatian situation. People should come to expect only kindness and goodness from us. The third group—"faithfulness, gentleness, self-control"—refers to personal qualities. We ought to be utterly reliable in all our dealings, easy to get along with, and in control of all our faculties.

Naturally there is no law against these sorts of qualities. The law exists to curb and restrain vice. Clearly there is no need of a deterrent here. This points up the impotence of the law. The law is able to expose and condemn the works of the flesh and thunder against them, but it is not able to produce the positive virtues which are their opposites. For that, people need to be controlled by the Holy Spirit.

And those who belong to Christ Jesus have cruci-
fied the flesh with its passions and desires. If we
live by the Spirit, let us also walk by the Spirit. Let
us have no self-conceit, no provoking of one an-
other, no envy of one another.
Brethren, if a man is overtaken in any trespass, you
who are spiritual should restore him in a spirit of
gentleness. Look to yourself, lest you too be temp-
ted. Bear one another's burdens, and so fulfil the
law of Christ. For if any one thinks he is some-
thing, when he is nothing, he deceives himself. But
let each one test his own work, and then his reason
to boast will be in himself alone and not in his
neighbor. For each man will have to bear his own
load. Galatians 5:24—6:5

How is a person to control the desires of his old nature and bear the fruit of the Spirit? Paul says there are two actions he must take, one negative, the other positive. There must be a painful repudiation of the old life (v. 24) and a resolute determination to walk by the Spirit (v. 25).

Earlier Paul spoke of our being crucified with Christ (2:20). But now he refers to a crucifixion which is done by us, not to us. We have put to death the old life. Paul is referring to our conversion when we turned away from sin and repudiated it altogether. The metaphor of crucifixion is very vivid. That form of death was hideously painful, and reserved for the worst criminals. If the flesh is something we have crucified, it must be something that deserves no better fate. It is not something to be treated politely with courtesy, but something to be executed pitilessly. Jesus Himself said, "If any man would come after me, let him deny himself and take up his cross and follow me" (Mark 8:34). Each of Christ's disciples is to be a condemned criminal, carrying his cross to the place of execution. We are, in this case, to take that wayward, selfish life and nail it to the cross, repudiating it completely. Death on the cross does not come at once. It is a gradual, agonizing death. The lower nature is not yet dead in any of us, but we are to keep it on the cross and let it die.

Paul's meaning is this. At conversion we took our old life, with all its sinful passions and desires, and nailed it to the cross. All right, Paul says, if we did that, we must leave it there to die. Holiness is a costly business. It does not come cheap. If sin continues to dominate our lives, it is either because we never truly repented or because we have not maintained our repentance. It is as if, having nailed the old nature to the cross, we keep returning to the place of execution, and long wistfully for it to be taken down from the cross. We all too readily try to coexist with the enemy. When temptations come, let us remember what we have done, crucified the flesh, and refuse to allow sin to come in. It is fatal to begin to reconsider how we are going to respond. We have declared war on the flesh and must not reopen negotiations on the subject. The issue is settled once and for all.

The positive action we must take is in regard to the Spirit. We cannot sanctify ourselves by our own effort. We need a divine resource outside of ourselves. Paul uses a different verb for "walking" in verse 25 than he did in verse 16. It contains the nuance of falling into step with someone. The verb is used of believers who "follow the example" of the faith Abraham had (Rom. 4:12). The idea here is that we ought deliberately to get into line with the Spirit. It is good to contrast this with something in verse 18. There Paul says the Spirit "leads" us, like a farmer herding cattle or a shepherd leading sheep. The Spirit is our leader. He asserts His desires in us against the desires of the old life. He puts gentle pressures upon us and guides in the way we should go. But that is not the complete picture. The Spirit is the path we should walk in, as well as the guide who shows us the way. The Spirit does the leading, but we do the walking. Our relation to His work is not wholly passive. We must decide to want Him to direct our lives. To "walk by the Spirit" in this sense is to walk along the path which He lays down.

Paul sets forth two principles of Christian holiness. We repudiate one path, the old life, in order to follow another. We turn from evil in order to occupy ourselves with what is right and good. We need to be ruthless in turning away from sin, and disciplined in turning to the things of the Spirit. Our decision to set our minds on the things of God will be apparent in everyday life. It will show up in the things we do, the books we read, and the friendships we make. Not only that, it will also transform our relationships with other people.

Being filled with the Spirit does not end in a private mystical experience. It opens the door to a new way of getting along with people. It sounds as if some of the Galatians were on a big ego-trip. Paul writes of self-conceit, provoking of one another, and envy (v. 26). Perhaps there was party spirit much like that which cropped up in the Corinthian congregation. At any rate, being controlled by the Spirit rules out all forms of ambitious rivalry and envy. There is a unity between these three attitudes. When we put ourselves first, we provoke others to show how superior they are. If that is impossible, we envy the other person and covet the gifts he has. Personal relations get poisoned through sin. The solution which can bring about healing in these situations is the Spirit filled life.

How does this work out in a practical situation? Paul gives us an example (v. 1). Here we have a person who has made a mistake. He may be speaking of a Judaizer who has realized the error of his ways and is penitent. In such a case, the spiritual person will not stand aside and take delight in the repentant sinner's mistake. Rather, he will be the first to move in and seek to help. The verb "restore" can mean mending a ripped net or setting a fractured bone. We are to help the person get back on the right track. The fruit of the Spirit in the lives of those walking by the Spirit will show up in this kind of action. Self-giving love is the sign of the fulness of the Spirit. We should be gentle in doing it because we are prone to making mistakes ourselves.

Now Paul enunciates the principle he has just illustrated. "Bear one another's burdens, and so fulfil the law of Christ." All of us have burdens, and God does not mean for us to carry them alone. Some people try to. They think it is a sign of fortitude to bear them and not bother other people with them. This is not a Christian attitude. We have been united to Christ in one body so that we can minister to one another. "If one member suffers, all suffer together; if one member is honored, all rejoice together" (I Cor. 12:26). On one occasion when Paul was terribly burdened, God sent Titus to comfort him (II Cor. 7:5, 6). God's comfort was not given to Paul simply through prayer and the Spirit, but through the companionship of a friend and the good news he brought with him. God intends for us to share our burdens with one another. The Judaizers were seeking to impose on the Galatians the "burden" of the law. They ought to be seeking to bear their burdens and so fulfil Christ's law.

The "law of Christ" is a striking phrase. The Galatian controversy over law must have led Paul to adopt this terminology. He is referring of course to the new commandment which Christ gave us (John 13:34; 15:12). Loving one another is the way to fulfil what God requires of us. We are called to be burden bearers. We live under a new kind of obligation—the unspectacular, even mundane, ministry of sharing people's burdens.

Self-sacrifice like this is incompatible with self-importance (v. 3). If we think a lot of our own importance, we will feel it beneath our dignity to stoop down to bear people's burdens. We must entertain a sane estimate of our own importance. The Christian needs to see he is nothing in his own right. He owes everything to Christ, who gave His life a ransom for many. When we look at it that way, we will not be too proud to share other people's burdens with them.

Instead of setting ourselves up as judges of others, Paul suggests that we take stock of ourselves (v. 4 f.). "Let each one test his own work." It is only to God that we are responsible for what we do. To Him we will give an account one day. The "load" Paul refers to in verse 5 is the weight of personal responsibility which no one can share with us. This is one burden we must carry alone—our responsibility to God on the day of judgment. There is thus no contradiction with verse 2. So, instead of looking down on others and comparing ourselves with them, we ought to ask what God has done in our lives and glory in that.

> *Let him who is taught the word share all good things with him who teaches. Do not be deceived; God is not mocked, for whatever a man sows, that he will also reap. For he who sows to his own flesh will from the flesh reap corruption; but he who sows to the Spirit will from the Spirit reap eternal life. And let us not grow weary in well-doing, for in due season we shall reap, if we do not lose heart. So then, as we have opportunity, let us do good to all men, and especially to those who are of the household of faith.* Galatians 6:6-10

In the midst of these general exhortations, Paul cites a familiar proverb: "Whatever a man sows, he shall also reap" (v. 7). This theme gives coherence to the passage. The harvest reaped bears a direct relation to the seed sown. This principle stands firm also in the moral and spiritual realms. Men may think they can escape its application, but they cannot. They may persist in ignoring God's Word and closing their eyes to the consequences, but in the end God will bring the harvest home.

Paul applies the principle first to the Christian ministry. The appropriate response of the pupil being taught God's truth is to give money in support of his teacher. In another place Paul writes: "If we have sown spiritual good among you, is it too much if we reap your material benefits?" (I Cor. 9:11). The reference may be to the "teaching elder" (I

Tim. 5:17). Though Paul did not raise support for himself, he did make a real effort to gather a collection for the needy saints in Jerusalem (Rom. 15:27).

This excellent principle can easily be abused. A minister, for example, may take his support without putting all his energies into the work. He might even seek to become rich from his ministry. Obviously he should not be in it to see what he can get out of it. He ought to throw himself into the ministry with the energy of a laboring man and sow good seed in the minds and hearts of his congregation.

The principle can also be abused from the other direction. Congregations abuse it when they use the fact of their support to muzzle the preacher and try to control his freedom in the gospel. They think that because they pay the piper, they should call the tune. The right relationship between pastor and people is one of "fellowship" or "sharing." The support the pastor receives is not his "pay." It is the people's sharing with him in return for his sharing with them.

The sowing and reaping principle applies also to the moral realm. What we become morally depends on what we sow. Sowing to the flesh means encouraging and pampering it, instead of crucifying it. Then if we do not grow in holiness, we should not be surprised. Holiness is a harvest that we reap. What we become depends largely on how we behave day after day. If we entertain impure thoughts, allow ourselves to become angry, wallow in self-pity, we are sowing to the flesh. Our character is formed by our conduct. Sowing to the Spirit, or sowing in the field of the Spirit, would be to cultivate our knowledge and experience of the things of God. As we foster good habits of devotion and prayer, as we busy ourselves in the work of the Lord, we are sowing to the Spirit.

There are two sowings and two harvests. If we sow to the flesh, we will reap corruption. Paul means more than simply moral decay. Corruption is the end of fallen human nature. The person who sows to the flesh will go from bad to worse, and finally perish. If, on the other hand, we sow to the Spirit, a process of spiritual and moral growth will begin, which will finally be consummated in eternal life and communion with God. If we wish to reap a harvest of holiness, we must studiously avoid sowing to the flesh (cf. 5:24) and concentrate our time and energies on sowing to the Spirit (cf. 5:25).

Finally Paul applies the principle to Christian philanthropy in general (v. 9 f.). If Paul tells men they cannot be saved by their good works, he also tells them they ought to do good deeds. We ought to be always on the lookout for the opportunity to show mercy and love. But the great danger which faces the spiritual farmer in this context is discouragement. It is easy to lose heart. Sacrificial Christian living is a tiring, exacting affair. None of us are immune from discouragement. Paul knew the same temptation: "Therefore, having this ministry by the mercy of God, we do not lose heart" (II Cor. 4:1). What we need to keep in mind, Paul says, is the certainty of harvest, which will come in God's own time. Too many of us are like children, expecting to sow and then reap on the same day! We need to cultivate a long-range view in the light of God's ultimate future.

Paul speaks here of good being done both to believers and nonbelievers. Helping members of the household of faith has priority, but it does not stop there. Like the Master, we ought to have in mind not only the sheep, but the not-yet-sheep. We have a special obligation toward fellow Christians because we have a special relation with them, and also because only if the Christian community is strong can it minister properly to the world.

Paul has applied the sowing and reaping principle to three spheres of the Christian life. The teacher who sows God's Word should reap a living from it. The believer who sows to the Spirit will reap eternal communion with God. The Christian philanthropist who sows good deeds will reap a good crop when the day of judgment comes. In none of these spheres is God mocked. The principle of sowing and reaping invariably operates.

Chapter Nine

the essence of christianity

*See with what large letters I am writing to you
with my own hand. It is those who want to make a
good showing in the flesh that would compel you
to be circumcised, and only in order that they
might not be persecuted for the cross of Christ.
For even those who receive circumcision do not
themselves keep the law, but they desire to have
you circumcised that they may glory in your flesh.
But far be it from me to glory except in the cross
of our Lord Jesus Christ, by which the world has
been crucified to me, and I to the world. For
neither circumcision counts for anything, nor uncircumcision, but a new creation. Peace and mercy
be upon all who walk by this rule, upon the Israel
of God. Henceforth let no man trouble me; for I
bear on my body the marks of Jesus. The grace of
our Lord Jesus Christ be with your spirit, brethren.
Amen.* Galatians 6:11-18

Many books have been written about the "essence of
Christianity." Usually they have been clever attempts to
reduce the Biblical faith to a single principle which would be
acceptable to the culture of the time. They were especially
popular in the nineteenth century when it was the custom to
interpret Christianity as religious moralism. It is refreshing to
be able to read Paul's final summary to the Galatians, in
which he tells us what the essence of Christianity really is.

Now the letter is almost over. Paul takes up the pen
himself to add the final comments. It was his custom to
employ a scribe in the writing of the epistles, and then bring

them to a close in his own handwriting (cf. II Thess. 3:17). The largeness of the script would be in contrast with the small, neat lettering of the professional scribe. Or, the large letters may be quite deliberate, a device to capture attention for some final important remarks. In them he pinpoints the vital issues at stake in this whole controversy.

Why in the last analysis were the Judaizers trying to have the Galatians circumcised? Because they wanted to "make a good showing in the flesh" (v. 12). Their concern was outward ceremonies and ecclesiastical statistics. It sounds as if they wished to add the Galatians to their list of converts so they could boast about it. A few hundred circumcisions a year was certainly something to boast about in some circles! Don't we hear of churches that boast in the number of baptisms in a similar manner? It is a natural tendency of the fallen heart to replace vital, inward religion with external, empty formalism.

Had we asked the Judaizers what they thought their motives were, the answer would have been a little different. They probably hoped to bridge the gap between Christianity and orthodox Judaism. As yet the division between the two movements had not become final. They thought that by getting the Gentiles to accept circumcision they would be able to set the minds of the Jews at ease and keep the lines of communication open with them. Unfortunately they did not see that they were falsifying the gospel by their actions. Paul says they were seeking to avoid persecution for the cross of Christ. He means that by compelling the Gentile believers to be circumcised they were adding a condition to salvation through Christ's cross other than simple faith. They made a religion of grace into a religion of works. The cross draws persecution because it cuts across all works-religion. The price the Judaizers were prepared to pay for communicating with the Jews was just too high.

The irony of the whole affair, Paul adds, is that even the people advocating circumcision are unable to keep the law perfectly (v. 13). They do not practice what they preach. They do not keep the law because it is impossible to do so. If the Judaizers themselves would only see their own inability to obey God perfectly, they would stop trying to pressure the Galatians to accept legalism. If the Judaizers are looking for something to glory in, Paul has a better suggestion.

Paul does not boast in circumcision or uncircumcision. He boasts only in the cross, which makes all such outward conditions and distinctions meaningless. What matters is not what we have done for ourselves, but what Christ has done for us. It is impossible to boast simultaneously in ourselves and in the cross. If we boast in what we have done to save ourselves, we will not be able to boast in what Christ has done to save us. We have to make a choice. The gospel invites us to renounce all boasting in our own achievements and to spend our lives boasting in the cross of Christ. The cross was absolutely central to Paul's theology and religious life. The essence of Christianity? What God has done for us in Christ, not what we have done for ourselves.

Because of the cross, the believer and the world part company. "The world has been crucified to me and I to the world." Before we were Christians it mattered a great deal what the world thought of us. Now all that matters is what God thinks of us in Jesus Christ. He has accepted us freely by His grace. Therefore the question whether a person has been circumcised or not is really unimportant. Is he a new creation through Christ (v. 15)? Religious ceremonies are outward acts of the flesh. They are important in that they signify inward reality, but they must not be substituted for it. What matters is the inward and invisible miracle performed by God in man himself.

Paul sets forth two great evangelical principles in defining for us the essence of Christianity. Christianity is not a religion of external ceremony, but something inward and spiritual. How common it has been in the history of religion for the worship of the heart to be debased into a superficial outward show. It was the sin of ancient Israel against which the prophets so vigorously protested (cf. Isa. 29:13). The great evangelical awakenings of modern times have been against the background of dead religious formalism. According to Paul, the outward distinctions are completely overshadowed by the overwhelming fact of the new creation in us.

Furthermore, Christianity is a religion of divine achievement, not human achievement. It is a matter of what God has done for us, not what we have done for ourselves. The Judaizers made a man's salvation dependent on his obedience to the law. They implied that he had to merit the favor and forgiveness of God by his own good works. Paul had to challenge this error vigorously. We are accepted in God's sight because of the cross of Christ. There is no place at all for human boasting.

To this Paul adds a short benediction. "Peace and mercy be upon all who walk by this rule, upon the Israel of God" (v. 16). His words are reminiscent of a psalm (125:5) in which the writer contrasts the crooked ways of the wicked with faithful Israel who trusts in the Lord. Paul is contrasting those who look to outward ceremonies for salvation with those who trust Christ alone. God's blessings are on those who walk by "this rule"; that is, according to the great evangelical principles Paul has just set forth. This is how a church can be sure of enjoying the favor of the Lord, by directing her life by the teachings of grace and the doctrine of the apostles. If the people boast in the cross of Christ, they can be sure of God's blessing.

Does Paul equate the church with Israel in this text (v. 16)? Many think he does. The "and" in the original can be taken either to indicate another object of God's blessing, or to qualify the believers more precisely as Israel. If Paul does identify Israel and the church here, it would be the boldest example in the New Testament of this. Certainly he believed that the church is an heir of Abraham's blessings (3:14) and in some sense his "offspring" (3:29). Elsewhere Paul writes, "We are the true circumcision, who worship God in spirit, and glory in Christ Jesus, and put no confidence in the flesh" (Phil. 3:3). The relevance of this to the Galatian situation would have been enormous. It would mean that the believing Gentiles who walked by this rule belonged to God's people, whereas the Judaizers, so proud of their Jewish heritage, did not.

Nevertheless, at this time in history, before the fall of Jerusalem, the term "Israel" had reference to ethnic Israel. Paul did not believe the church had replaced Israel. Romans 9–11 is devoted to explaining how God intended to fulfil His promises to them. It is more likely that Paul wishes to couple two groups as the objects of God's blessing: the Gentiles who believe the gospel and the Jewish Christians who recognize the unimportance of circumcision. By so doing, these Jewish believers prove themselves to be true Israelites, members of the faithful remnant. It would be a tactful comment for Paul to make just to ensure that the Jewish Christians did not think he grouped them together with the Judaizers.

Having concluded his discussion, Paul makes an appeal that the Judaizers stop harassing him. "Henceforth let no man trouble me; for I bear on my body the marks of Jesus." His language is striking. In answer to the Judaizers who kept insisting on outward marks on the body, Paul says he has all the marks he needs. What are these distinguishing marks to which he refers? The word he uses, *stigmata,* referred to the brand marks that were put on a slave to indicate who owned him, a kind of tattoo. The marks of Jesus which Paul carried on his body must have been the scars received in the service of Christ. We know something of the persecutions he suffered (II Cor. 4:7-12). These were public evidence of his complete allegiance to Jesus. As a Jew, Paul also bore the mark of circumcision. But he is prouder of the marks he received in preaching the gospel than the one which marked him as a son of Abraham. These are the marks we ought to covet, those which are inflicted on account of our faithfulness to the gospel of Christ.

In closing Paul invokes the grace of God to be with them. This was, after all, the whole point of the letter. It was the principle that was being seriously threatened. His final prayer is that divine grace may come again to dominate the thinking of his Galatian converts. "Amen"—so be it!

epilogue

Galatians really gets to the heart of what the Christian faith is. At first sight the benediction with which Paul ends his epistle seems plain and unadorned. But on closer examination its full beauty shines forth. The text actually opens up for us what Galatians is about.

1. The GRACE of our Lord Jesus Christ.

In singling out the grace of God, Paul recalls for us the entire sweep of the letter. Salvation is by God's achievement, not man's. He first mentioned grace in the greeting (1:3-4), where he connected it with the atoning death of Jesus. God's grace is epitomized and rendered operative in the finished work of Christ. Salvation then is a matter of believing, not achieving.

Grace is the matter which excites Paul so in the polemical section (chaps. 1–2). If any preconditions are demanded in the matter of salvation, that is another gospel. Justification is by faith and not by works. That is the apostolic message. Paul urges his readers to submit themselves to the teaching of the apostles, which magnifies the grace of God.

The central section of the epistle is devoted to proving that salvation by grace is the teaching of the Old Testament as well. The letter ends with the fact that holiness can be attained only in the life of the person who allows himself to be controlled by the Spirit.

The Epistle to the Galatians clearly articulates the free grace of God apart from human works and based on the finality and sufficiency of Christ's work on the cross. What a relief to be assured of this! If we know our hearts, we know that we have failed to meet God's standards. And yet we know that God is gracious still.

2. The grace of our LORD JESUS CHRIST.

Paul gives Jesus His full title. Jesus, which means Savior, is the Lord, who owns, governs, and protects us, and the Christ, the anointed of God, our high priest and mediator. No other epistle of Paul's is so dominated by the central importance of Christ. His deepest concern in the first section is the integrity of Christ's gospel. We are not dealing here with matters of merely human authority or opinion. It is the gospel of Christ which is at stake. Paul's entire sense of authority is bound up with the relationship he had with Him.

Several times in the letter Paul explains why it is that faith in Christ saves a person. "He gave himself for our sins to deliver us" (1:4). Later on Paul refers to the redemption by Christ's blood. "Christ redeemed us from the curse of the law, having become a curse for us" (3:13). Christ saves sinners by putting Himself in their place. This decisive fact explains why we should boast in nothing else (6:14).

In addition, Paul emphasizes that we can have an intimate personal relationship with Christ. We are *in Christ*. Christ sustains a spiritual relationship with those He has redeemed. This very fact proves Jesus Christ is the divine Son of God. No merely human religious leader could be said to do that. Jesus Christ has become the very center of our lives. He lives in us (2:20).

Paul's gospel was the gospel of Christ (1:7). Just as his life was centered on Christ, so was his message (2:16). It was Christ whom Paul "placarded" before the Galatians as crucified (3:1). To believers in Christ all the promised blessings of God will be fulfilled (3:14, 22).

Jesus Christ is the center of the gospel because God accepts us on His account. We are not saved because we are better than other people. We should have no illusions about our personal goodness. We ought to despair of pleasing God by our own efforts, so that we may trust completely in Jesus Christ.

3. Be with your SPIRIT, brethren.

The Galatian Christians were being tempted to treasure the outward mark of circumcision and boast in it. It was a purely external badge of religious formalism. The reason Paul took Titus with him to Jerusalem was to force this issue. Circumcision could not be required of him because God had fully accepted him in Christ. Church membership functions in very much the same way today. What really matters is the vital relationship of the whole person with Christ.

Paul shows excellent balance in this matter. He boasts neither in circumcision nor in uncircumcision. Christ alone is what matters, and the vital union with Him which issues in righteousness (5:5-6). How often Christians who are proud they don't do something are perfectly matched by others who are proud they do! Paul is only concerned about the new creation which God is bringing about (6:15). Christ effects in the believer a total renewal, a foretaste of the renovation of all things. Christianity is a religion of the future. We wait for the hope of righteousness. As renewed men, therefore, we should be preparing for that day by actions of faith which concretely testify to and anticipate that coming hour.

4. Be with your spirit, BRETHREN.

It is impressive that at the close of a hot and polemical epistle Paul should address the Galatians warmly as his brothers. The beginning of the letter was outstanding for its omission of all commendation and praise. Paul launched right away into a denunciation of the false teachers and their all-too-willing pupils. Later on Paul wondered whether a spell had not in fact been cast upon them. They were foolish indeed. He also refers to the fact that they now regard him as their enemy rather than their friend. So his calling them his brethren here is impressive. Despite the hard feelings, and even though they were wavering in their Christian commitment, Paul generously takes them to be his brothers. He visits them with tender affection despite their ill-treatment of him. His love for them does not fail, even though their doctrinal orthodoxy and their love for him are in doubt. He loves them still. There is something to be learned here in our attitudes to other Christians. No one could accuse Paul of being a theological relativist! Truth mattered greatly to him. Yet he was charitable toward those Christians who differed even seriously with him. They too belonged to Christ.